Japan is the first Asian country to develop a strong and viable democracy although she had no democratic tradition. Her system of government and politics was thoroughly authoritarian and this was consistent with the social and political values the Japanese held as good. Yet the transition from authoritarianism to democracy was rapid. It makes an interesting study as to how Japan overcame the apparently insurmountable obstacles of authoritarianism to embrace the alien ideas of democracy.

The present form of the Government of Japan is based on the Constitution of 1947. This Constitution was adopted as an amendment to its predecessor—the Meiji Constitution of 1889. But in fact, it was a total revision which brings about revolutionary changes in the governmental structure. Foremost among them are: the transfer of sovereign power from the Emperor to the people, the supremacy of the legislature, separation of powers and the guarantee of fundamental human rights. Another revolutionary change is the renunciation of "war as a sovereign right of the nation and the threat or use of force as means of settling international disputes."

The author of this volume seeks to deal with these changes.

by Niranjan Bhuinya
International Organisations

PARLIAMENTARY DEMOCRACY IN JAPAN

Niranjan Bhuinya

Mr. Niranjan Bhuinya (b. 1940) studied at the University of Calcutta. After having a brilliant academic career, he is now teaching Political Science in Ramakrishna Mission Vidyamandir, Howrah.

BARNES & NOBLE BOOKS—NEW YORK
(A DIVISION OF HARPER & ROW PUBLISHERS, INC.)

Published in the U.S.A., 1972 by
HARPER & ROW PUBLISHERS, INC.,
BARNES & NOBLE IMPORT DIVISION

ISBN 389 04653 1

Published in India by
Associated Publishing House
New Market, Karol Bagh, New Delhi-5

PRINTED IN INDIA
PRINTED AND PUBLISHED BY R. K. PAUL FOR
ASSOCIATED PUBLISHING HOUSE, NEW DELHI-5

To
the memory of those Japanese nationals who
fought and died for their motherland

Japan's National Anthem

"Kimigayo"—"The Reign of Our Emperor"

Ten thousand years of happy reign be thine:
Rule on, my lord, till what are pebbles now
By ages united to mighty rocks shall grow
Whose venerable sides the moss doth line.

Translation by B.H. Chamberlain

Preface

THE PRESENT form of the Government of Japan is based on the Constitution of 1947 which was adopted as an amendment to its predecessor—the Meiji Constitution of 1889. But, in fact, it was a total revision which brings about revolutionary changes in the governmental structure. Foremost among them are: the transfer of sovereign power from the Emperor to the people, the supremacy of the legislature, separation of powers and the guarantee of fundamental human rights. Another revolutionary change is the renunciation of "war as a sovereign right of the nation and the threat or use of force as means of settling international disputes".

The author of this volume seeks to deal with these changes. He humbly submits that this book is not meant for those who claim to be experts on modern Japan. It will be in the entire satisfaction of the author if it serves the needs of the average students of Asian governments.

The author acknowledges his debt to his teachers, students and colleagues and also to his friend Sri Satadru Shovan Chakravarti, M. A., who inspired and encouraged him to prepare this book. The author is particularly grateful to the office of the Consulate-General of Japan, Calcutta, for supplying him a number of copies of *Facts about Japan* and a few documents.

Niranjan Bhuinya

Contents

Preface   *Page vii*

1. Road to Democracy   1

2. Philosophy of the Constitution   6

3. Basic Principles of the Constitution   10
   Constitution—the Supreme law of the land;
   Popular Sovereignty; Parliamentary Democracy;
   Direct Democracy; Fundamental Human Rights;
   Renunciation of War

4. The Emperor   23
   The Emperor under the Constitution of 1889;
   Why the Emperor? The Emperor Under the New
   Constitution

5. The Cabinet   37
   Nature of the Cabinet; Composition of the Cabinet;
   Functions of the Cabinet; The Prime Minister

6. The Diet   48
   The House of Representatives; The House of
   Councillors; Qualifications of the Members of
   the Diet; The Speaker and the Vice-Speaker;
   Immunities of the Diet-members; Session of
   the Diet; Functions of the Diet; Relation
   Between the Two Houses of the Diet.

7. The Judiciary   62
   The Supreme Court; Inferior Courts; Public
   Procurators; No Extraordinary Tribunal; Popular
   Review of Judges; Independence of the Judiciary;
   Judicial Review

8. Rights and Duties of the People   73

9. Political Parties   79

10. Local Self-Government   90

Appendices

1. Chronological outline of some of the most   95
   important events in the history of modern Japan
   during the last 100 years

2. National Governmental Structure   97

3. National Administrative Organs   98

4. Party Positions in the Diet as on January 29, 1967   100

5. The Constitution of Japan   101

   Selected Bibliography   117

   Index   119

If we can bring democracy to Japan and make it work, all of Asia will look toward this land. History shows that democratic nations do not wage wars of aggression.

—General MacArthur

CHAPTER 1

Road to Democracy

Japan's peaceful democratic revolution was born of a lost war.

—John M. Maki

J A P A N is the first Asian country to develop a strong and viable democracy although she had no democratic tradition. Her system of government and politics was thoroughly authoritarian and this was consistent with the social and political values the Japanese held as good. Yet the transition from authoritarianism to democracy was rapid. It makes an interesting study as to how Japan overcame the apparently insurmountable obstacles of authoritarianism to embrace the alien ideas of democracy.

In Great Britain democracy developed through the centuries. That is to say the growth of democracy in Great Britain was gradual and evolutionary. In Japan, on the other hand, democracy did not undergo evolutionary growth. The case was one of changing the authoritarian structure of government to a democratic one. The special circumstances which combined to make possible this peaceful democratic revolution are: a lost war, the chaos and dislocations of defeat, an enlightened occupation, a society equipped with the basic institutions of the modern state, and a population generally willing to reject the discredited authoritarianism and to embark on the construction of a new democracy.[1]

Japan's social and political history from 1600 to 1867 reveals the domination of a single family. During this period the Tokugawa family enjoyed unchallenged political supremacy and brought the Japanese system of feudalism to its highest point of development. The feudal lords, several hundreds in

[1] Maki, John M., *Government and Politics in Japan*, p. 8.

number, and in control of their own estates, were largely independent though loyal to the Tokugawa government. The society was strictly hierarchical. The warrior class belonged to the highest stratum of society, followed by the other social classes—the peasants, artisans and the merchants in the descending order. Japan's economy was mainly agrarian though a commercial sector operated by the merchant class existed side by side. But this class was insignificant in terms of political power.

The Tokugawa government controlled the lives and activities of all the members of the society through the monopoly of arms. Naturally there was, and could be, no individual freedom. For more than 250 years the Tokugawa family was in power in Japan. This demonstrates the traditional subservience of the Japanese to their rulers.

However, the third quarter of the 19th century witnessed profound changes in the socio-political set-up. The emergence of an industrial economy and wider contacts with the western world challenged the authoritarian structure of the traditional Japanese society. The leaders of the Tokugawa family were aware of these developments. But in spite of their brilliancy in statesmanship and strategy they were unable to direct or control these developments. Under the stress and strain of the new circumstances the Tokugawa regime collapsed and the last of the Tokugawas, Keiki, surrendered his office to Emperor Meiji in 1867.

With the end of feudalism a modern nation-state with all its essential features was gradually coming into being.

Japan had its first modern constitution only in the year 1889, that is, 22 years after the collapse of the Tokugawa regime. This constitution, which remained the fundamental law of Japan until 1947, was drafted on the models of the autocratic and monarchical constitutions of Prussia and Austria. It is not unnatural, therefore, that the fundamental principle of the constitution was the absolute sovereignty of the Emperor. There was no democratic separation of powers, no system of checks and balances. All powers—legislative, administrative and judicial—were made to emanate from the Emperor.

In practice, however, the Cabinet was the most dominant organ of the government of Japan. It was responsible only to the Emperor and not to the people or their representatives. In the Cabinet again, the War and Navy Ministries were the most predominant. By custom and by ordinance only a general or an admiral could be a Minister of War or the Navy. "If a Prime Minister could not find a general or an admiral to hold these offices he could not form or maintain a Cabinet, and professional spirit was so strong that no general or admiral would serve as Army or Navy Minister in a Cabinet whose policy was strongly disapproved of by his Service. Thus the Army and Navy staff were able to exert a continual and at times decisive influence on policy by withdrawing, or threatening to withdraw, the Service Ministers from a Cabinet".[1] The influence and control of the services over policy matters was largely responsible for the development of authoritarianism and militarism in Japan from 1930 onward.

This trend towards authoritarianism and militarism continued unabated until the end of World War II. Japan's military involvement in a series of war from 1894-95 right up to the beginning of World War II helped the protagonists of war to extend the tentacles of authoritarianism over every aspect of the .lives of the people and to inculcate in them the spirit of aggressive militarism.

In this process the bureaucrats and the financial cliques cooperated with the military. There was no responsible government, no free election, no freedom of thought, expression, association or assembly. All efforts directed towards liberalism and democracy and towards undermining authoritarianism were suppressed by the police. However, there were no excesses and this is because loyalty to the Emperor, who symbolized the state, was still considered by the average Japanese a virtue.

It must be clear, therefore, that before a democratic society could be established in Japan these features of authoritarianism must be eliminated first.

The devastating war and Japan's crushing defeat filled the minds of the people with revulsion against the administration which was dominated by the military. At the same time it aroused in them a deep desire for freedom, democracy and liberalism. Here lies the secret of Japan's peaceful democratic revolution.

[1] Churchill, *War Memoirs, ii,* p. 455.

The United States was determined from the very beginning to terminate "the influence of the military leaders who have brought Japan to the present brink of disaster"[1] and to introduce a workable democracy in Japan which, it was believed, would prevent Japan from embarking on military adventure in future.

The hope for a peaceful Japan, it was understood, lies, first of all, in a thorough-going reconstruction of her political system and the establishment of a popular government in which the leaders of the nation can be held responsible to the people rather than to the Emperor.

The Potsdam Declaration stated in clear and unambiguous terms: "There must be eliminated for all time the authority and influence of those who have deceived and misled the people of Japan into embarking on world conquest, for we insist that a new order of peace, security, and justice will be impossible until irresponsible militarism is driven from the world."

At the same time the Declaration guaranteed the establishment of freedom of speech, of religion, and of thought as well as respect for the fundamental human rights. However, Japan's leaders were very much concerned about the future of the Emperor. So an additional guarantee had to be issued on behalf of the Allied Powers: "The ultimate form of government of Japan shall, in accordance with the Potsdam Declaration, be established by the freely expressed will of the people."

Accordingly, the occupation policy for Japan was directed to the achievement of two main objectives: (a) to secure a peace-loving Japan which will not again disturb the peace and security of the world; and (b) to establish a democratic responsible government in Japan.

These objectives are to be achieved by complete disarmament and demilitarization of Japan and through democratisation of Japan's social and political systems and of her economy.

The occupation in its first directive sought the "Removal of Restrictions on Political, Civil and Religious Liberties." The Emperor was reduced from the position of absolute ruler to that of a constitutionally limited monarch. The armed forces were demobilized and the military command was dissolved.

[1] Policy Statement by President Truman released on May 8, 1945.

The authoritarian structure was replaced "by a system consisting of an executive branch with greatly reduced powers, a legislative branch supreme within the government, and a judicial branch created to protect the rights and freedoms of the people."[1]

Within a few years of occupation Japan developed a party system to run the representative government. A new economic order was also created to provide the foundation for a new democracy. Thus was made the set ready for transition from authoritarianism to democracy. This transition was planned and executed by the Occupation Government. But the Japanese people in general welcomed this transition partly because of the imposing character of the occupation authority and partly because of their complete disillusionment with the military authoritarianism.

[1] Maki, *op. cit.*, p. 51.

CHAPTER 2

Philosophy of the Constitution

It is an admitted maxim, in the ordinary course of the administration of justice, that the preamble of a statute is a key to open the mind of the makers as to the mischiefs which are to be remedied and the objects which are to be accomplished by the provisions of the statute. . . .

—Justice Story of the U.S. Supreme Court

THE PREAMBLE to a Constitution is no part of it, and has no binding force, yet it is the key to the understanding of the document and the proper yardstick by which to judge its merit. The Preamble indicates the purpose and the principles which the Constitution seeks to promote. It is, in other words, indicative of the philosophy of the Constitution and also of the source from which the Constitution derives its authority.

Here lies the importance and the significance of the Preamble to a Constitution.

Echoing the Preamble to the Constitution of the United States, the Preamble to the new Constitution of Japan starts with the words: "We, the Japanese people", emphasizing thereby the ultimate sovereignty of the people—undoubtedly a fundamental departure from the past. No more the sovereign power shall be held by the Emperor. The new Constitution shifts the emphasis from the Emperor to the people who are now sovereign and supreme in all that concerns them.

The Preamble refers to a "universal principle" of mankind upon which the new Constitution is based: "Government is a sacred trust of the people, the authority for which is derived from the people, the powers of which are exercised by the representatives of the people, and the benefits of which are enjoyed by the people".

This principle implies that the government shall be not only responsible but also responsive to the needs of the people. And

6

since the benefits of the government are open to all, it shall be a government not only by the people, but also for the people.

But the most dramatic—and we should say the most reassuring part of the Preamble—is the firm resolve of the people to secure for themselves and their posterity "the fruits of peaceful cooperation with all nations and the blessings of liberty throughout this land," and never again to be visited "with the horrors of war through the action of government."

The significance of this resolution will be understood if we keep in mind how Japan was drawn to the vortex of war through the thoughtless action and adventurism of the government and the magnitude of devastation and the horrors of war experienced by the millions of Japanese.

The Preamble confirms the desire of the Japanese people for peace for all time and their awareness of the high ideals controlling human relationship. They are determined to preserve their security and existence, trusting in the justice and faith of the peace-loving peoples of the world. They desire to occupy an honoured place in an international society striving for the preservation of peace, and the banishment of tyranny and slavery, oppression and intolerance for all time from the earth. They recognize that all the peoples of the world have the right to live in peace, free from fear and want.

This at once reminds us of the Preamble to the Charter of the U. N. which says that the people of the United Nations are determined "to save succeeding generations from the scourge of war ... to practise tolerance and live together in peace with one another as good neighbours and to unite our strength to maintain international peace and security. ... "

The new generations of Japan thus pledged their faith in the basic purposes of the U. N. in early 1947 and their determination to be worthy of full membership of the world organization of which Japan became a member on December 16, 1956.

Japan's determination to live in peace can be properly appreciated if we keep in mind her imperialist missions, her ambition to establish her hegemony over the whole of South and South-East Asia—which was, of course, shattered,—and her long aggressive war with China, her treacherous and suicidal attack on Pearl Harbour which forced the United States into the war and extended both the scale and dimension of the war. All these steps were indicative of Japan's "oppression and intolerance".

Now, she is determined to banish "tyranny and slavery, oppression and intolerance for all time from the earth" and recognizes "for all peoples of the world" "the right to live in peace, free from fear and want."

This is an assurance to the peace-loving peoples of the world that no longer shall Japan cultivate her fanatical fighting spirit, which was systematically developed in her people by the wartime government, and that she will maintain an honourable relation based on faith and justice with the nations of the world.

The Preamble to the new Constitution thus holds out the promise of the growth and development of a peaceful and trustworthy Japan, no longer obsessed with her superiority of race and the spirit of domination—worthy of full membership in the family of nations.

Here it may not be out of place to quote in part the Preamble to the Constitution of 1889 promulgated in the name of Emperor Meiji, the grandfather of the present-Emperor Hirohito: "Having by virtue of the glories of our Ancestors, ascended the throne of a lineal succession unbroken for ages eternal; desirring to promote the welfare of, and to give development to the moral and intellectual faculties of Our beloved subjects, the very same that have been favoured with the benevolent care and affectionate vigilance of our Ancestors, and hoping to maintain the prosperity of the state, in concert with Our people and with their support, we hereby promulgate in pursuance of our Imperial Rescript . . . a fundamental law of state, to exhibit the principles, by which we are to be guided in Our conduct, and to point out to what Our descendants and Our subjects and their descendants are for ever to conform."

This may be read with the pledge of the Japanese in war time when reactionary nationalism rose to a fever heat:

"We, the subjects of His Imperial Majesty the Emperor shall offer everything we have for the sake of His Imperial Majesty the Emperor, we shall extend the august virtue of His Imperial Majesty to all corners of the world; we shall certainly win this war by embracing and protecting the Imperial throne; we shall resolutely and absolutely worship His Imperial Majesty the Emperor; in reverent acceptance of His Imperial Edict we shall abide by it."

The patriotism of the Japanese and their love of country became "intricately bound up with the all-pervading authority of a theocratic Emperor. The Imperial myths have become part and parcel of the superstitions, religious beliefs and social customs, which together form the base for Japan's extreme nationalism."[1]

The Preamble to the new Constitution, as we have already seen, speaks in a different tone. It vibrates with the spirit of a new generation imbibed with a new spirit of "live and let live". It is gratifying to note that Japan is out to extricate her from her ancient moorings.

[1] Johnstone, W. C., *The Future of Japan*, p. 87.

CHAPTER 3

Basic Principles of the Constitution

Stereotypes such as totalitarian-democratic, federal-unitary, presidential-parliamentary, monarchical-republican, and so forth, seem hopelessly inadequate for describing the dynamic process of change in Japan.

—Ardath W. Burks

T H E J A P A N E S E Constitution of 1947, although "filled with ideas and concepts almost completely foreign to Japanese history, tradition and values", provides Japan with a workable governmental system and is the supreme law of the land. It is supreme over all organs of the national government. Its provisions, so far as they go, are binding on every one from the Emperor down to an ordinary man in the street.

Article 98 of the Constitution lays down: "This Constitution shall be the supreme law of the nation and no law, ordinance, imperial rescript or other act of government, or part thereof, contrary to the provisions hereof, shall have legal force or validity."

Article 99 obliges the Emperor or the Regent as well as Ministers of State, members of the Diet, judges and all other public officials to respect and uphold this Constitution. In the Preamble to the Constitution the people "reject and revoke all Constitutions, laws, ordinances and rescripts in conflict herewith."

This reminds us of Article VI paragraph 2 of the American Constitution which says: "This Constitution . . . shall be the supreme law of the land; and the judges in every state shall be bound thereby, anything in the Constitution or laws of any state to the contrary notwithstanding."

Popular Sovereignty

The old Constitution of the Empire of Japan was based on the principle of absolute sovereignty of the Emperor. The

Preamble to the Constitution says: "The rights of sovereignty of state, we have inherited from our Ancestors, and we shall bequeath them to our descendants." Article IV of the Constitution lays down: "The Emperor is the head of the Empire, combining in Himself the rights of sovereignty, and exercises them, according to the provisions of the present Constitution."

The new Constitution of Japan marks a fundamental departure from this. It recognizes the principle of popular sovereignty and destroys old principle of imperial sovereignty.

But the Constitution deals with this principle very casually. No independent Article is devoted to the sovereignty of the people and the only reference we get to this principle is in Article 1 of the Constitution which deals with the position of the Emperor. This Article says: "The Emperor shall be the symbol of the state and of the unity of the people with whom resides sovereign power."

The Preamble to the Constitution, however, says: "We, the Japanese people, acting through our duly elected representatives in the National Diet . . . do proclaim that sovereign power resides with the people and do firmly establish this Constitution." Here we have an echo of the Preamble to the Constitution of the United States which says: "We the people of the United States . . . do ordain and establish this Constitution for the United States of America." The late Professor Kazuo of Ohio State University observed: "These are most explicit expressions of the doctrine of popular sovereignty, a doctrine completely alien to Japanese thought."[1]

The Preamble to the Japanese Constitution further elaborates the principle: "Government is a sacred trust of the people, the authority for which is derived from the people, the powers of which are exercised by the representatives of the people, and the benefits of which are enjoyed by the people."

"This, incidentally", says Maki, "was one of the principal passages in the Constitution that sounded as if it had been translated from a foreign language, so alien did it seem in the light of traditional Japanese political thought."[2]

In the Indian Constitution also no independent article in the enacting portion declares that all powers are derived from the

[1] Quoted by Burks, *The Government of Japan*, p. 18.
[2] Maki, John M., *The Government and Politics in Japan*, p. 85.

people. Yet, the words "we, the people of India", as found in the Preamble, are taken to emphasize the ultimate sovereignty of the people. In other words, the Constitution establishes a system of government based on popular consent. "Unlike totalitarian constitutions, it postulates the capacity of men for self-government. It rests on the proposition that to follow the freely given judgment of the whole people is safer, if not always wiser, than to let the ultimate determination of public policy rest in the hands of any one who is beyond the reach of popular accountability".[1]

Although the Constitution is based on the principle of popular sovereignty it does not provide for direct popular government. The principle of popular sovereignty means that the government derives its authority from the people, that it is both representative and responsible. It is representative because the people freely choose their representatives to formulate their will in terms of law; it is responsible because the people can control their representatives directly or indirectly.

Of course, it can be argued, and quite rightly, that the men who drafted this Constitution were not, in fact, the representatives of the people, and that the Constitution was not approved by the people in a referendum. The Constitution was drafted in deep secrecy and in great haste by a group of foreigners. To quote Maki: "A combined crew of army and navy officers and civilians of varied background—lawyers, writers, professors, civil servants and a few without any professional experience who had gone into the services directly from college—was given the responsibility of drafting what was technically to be only a revision of the existing constitution, but actually was a completely new one."[2]

The draft of the Constitution was no doubt discussed by the Diet in all its aspects but it could not effect any change in the fundamental principles embodied in the draft. The Diet approved the Constitution on October 7, 1946, and it came into force on May 3, 1947. The Constitution was warmly supported by a substantial majority of the people as "a highly desirable, indeed indispensable, foundation for a going system of democracy". As

[1] Munro (with reference to the U.S. Constitution).
[2] *Ibid.*, p. 79.

Maki says: "It was the occupation that originated, directed, and obviously controlled the drafting, the content and the process of approval of the new Constitution. But it must also be noted that the Japanese role was active, however restricted."[1]

The Communists, however, were opposed to the new Constitution because they wanted the Emperor to be tried as a war criminal and the establishment of a People's Republic in Japan. But the overwhelming majority was in favour of the retention of the Throne and they approved the new Constitution as if it was their own making.

One of the principal reasons, it is believed in certain quarters, for the unpopularity of the Communists in Japan is their opposition to, and occasional attacks upon, the Throne. Critics of the Constitution, however, argue that since the Emperor is the symbol of the state, deriving his position from the will of the people with whom resides the sovereign power, Japan, srtictly speaking, is not a constitutional monarchy but a republic.

Here, it may not be wholly out of place to draw an analogy with the Soviet Constitution. Unlike the constitutions of Western democracies and those modelled on them, the Soviet Constitution speaks, not in the name of the people, but in the name of the workers and peasants, as if the workers and peasants make the whole people. The Constitution, therefore, offers enough scope for speculation as to the place of professional groups— doctors, engineers, lawyers, teachers and shopkeepers—in the scheme of government. These professional groups cannot be excluded from the people, on the other hand, they certainly cannot be identified with the workers and peasants. Either they do not exist, which is an absurd assumption, or they exist without any political influence.

Parliamentary Democracy

The Potsdam Declaration issued by President Truman and Prime Minister Churchill on July 26, 1945, called for the establishment of a "peacefully inclined and responsible government" in accordance with the "freely expressed will of the Japanese people". Japan could no longer be allowed to have

[1] Munro, *op. cit.*, p. 80.

an irresponsible and authoritarian government. Rather the
government was to be made responsible to the people and responsive to their needs.

This was the part of a larger and wider programme of dest-
roying the authoritarian structure and of keeping Japan permanently out of aggressive wars.

That the Constitution envisages a responsible government is
clear both from the Preamble to the Constitution and from
Articles 66 and 69. It is stated in the Preamble: "Government
is a sacred trust of the people, the authority for which is derived
from the people, the powers of which are exercised by the
representatives of the people and the benefits of which are enjoyed by the people."

Article 66 of the Constitution says: "The Cabinet, in the
exercise of executive power, shall be collectively responsible to
the Diet." Cabinet responsibility is further elaborated in Article 69: "If the House of Representatives passes a no-confidence
motion, or rejects a confidence resolution, the Cabinet shall
resign en masse, unless the House of Representatives is dissolved within ten (10) days."

The Constitution was prepared under American influence;
it was even drafted by the Americans. It may be an interesting query why the Americans did not think in terms of
Presidential executive. They have no monarchical tradition
and naturally they cannot be expected to have any affection
for the Emperor. Rather their dissatisfaction was demonstrated
by the enemy Press and government spokesmen during the war.
"They touched on his possible personal responsibility for
Japanese aggression and consequently his presumed guilt as a
war criminal, his role in the creation of the fanatical fighting
spirit of the Japanese, and the necessity for the elimination of
the imperial institution as a part of the programme of making
the Japanese a peace-loving people."[1]

But it was clearly understood by the Occupation Government
that whoever might be charged with war guilt, the Emperor
must not be the one. "The reverence for the Emperor is almost
unbelievable. . . . Furthermore, it is unfathomable since it is an

[1] Maki, *op. cit.*, p. 64.

emotional and practically a religious manifestation. . . . Emperor is necessary emotionally to the Japanese just as the Crown is to the Britons."[1]

Therefore, whoever else might be, the Emperor could not be made the target of vengeance. Moreover, the myth was to be created that the Constitution had its Japanese origin. The elimination of the Emperor would only destroy this myth. The Emperor, therefore, was to continue as the head of state thus linking the old and new Japan and he could be fit in only in a parliamentary set-up without causing any political friction.

Theodore McNelly writes on this: "There was much criticism that the Emperor was not indicted and tried. The reason usually given was that the Emperor was not constitutionally responsible in the Japanese system—he was simply a figure-head, and in spite of his personal views he had to do as his advisers told him. It was widely believed that the Americans spared the Emperor because his authority was necessary for administering the country and because his indictment might arouse popular opposition to the occupation."[2]

Direct Democracy

Institutions of direct democracy are: referendum, initiative, and recall. The American federal Constitution does not provide for any such devices although in some of the states of the Union these institutions still form a part of the political life of the people. Under the Indian Constitution also no obligation of the legislature to refer a piece of legislation to the people or the right of the people to initiate proposals for legislation or to call back their representatives have been admitted.

In this respect, the Japanese Constitution marks a departure. All constitutional amendments approved by the Diet must be submitted to the people in a special referendum and shall require affirmation by the majority of voters. Only comparable example is found under the Swiss Constitution where all constitutional amendments must compulsorily be referred to the people and

[1] Chistoshiyanaga, *Japanese People and Politics*, p. 130.
[2] McNelly, Theodore, *Contemporary Government of Japan*, p. 34.

also all treaties for 15 years or for an indefinite period of time. But whereas the Swiss people can initiate ordinary legislation and even proposals for constitutional amendments and by a specified number of voters demand that an ordinary legislation be referred to them, the Japanese Constitution does not recognize all these rights. The people cannot initiate amendment proposals nor even proposals for ordinary legislation and they cannot also demand that an ordinary legislation be referred to them by the Diet.

But, in another respect the Japanese enjoy more power. They have got the power to review the appointment of the judges of the Supreme Court and also the power to dismiss them. This is undoubtedly a unique feature of the new Japanese Constitution.

Moreover, the Japanese Constitution brings the people in closer relationship with the government and gives them a precedence over it. This is clear from Article 15 of the Constitution which says: "The people have the inalienable right to choose their public officials and to dismiss them.

"All public officials are servants of the whole community and not of any group thereof. Universal adult suffrage is guaranteed with regard to the election of public officials."

Previously, the public officials were the masters of the people, servants of the Emperor and responsible to him alone. From now on they shall be servants of the people and the people their masters.

In Great Britain even now all public officials, including the Chief of the Government, the Prime Minister, are Her Majesty's servants and legally at least she has the power to dismiss all of them. But even this fiction is not to be allowed under the new Constitution of Japan. According to Maki, "The provision that government officials shall be 'servants' of the people was designed to undermine the entrenched bureaucracy that formed one pillar of the authoritarian structure. The bureaucracy is still powerful. . . . However, the fact remains that public officials . . . are no longer representatives of an omnipotent executive with all its authority and force behind them. They are now subject to the pressures of the legislative branch and of a diligent public opinion."[1]

[1] Maki, *op. cit.*, p. 109.

Fundamental Human Rights

The new Japanese Constitution incorporates a truly imposing list of rights for individual Japanese citizens. Article 11 of the Constitution says: "The people shall not be prevented from enjoying any of the fundamental human rights." Article 13 lays down: "All of the people shall be respected as individuals. Their right to life, liberty and the pursuit of happiness shall, to the extent that it does not interfere with the public welfare, be the supreme consideration in legislation and in other governmental affairs."

The rights guaranteed by the Constitution shall be "eternal and inviolate". Here is another instance of Western influence on the Constitution. There was nothing like the "eternal and inviolate" rights of the people under the old Constitution. Rights of the people were never treated as sacred. They could be violated, abridged, curtailed or even mutilated not only by statutory enactments but "through loopholes in the law and legal fictions". The new Constitution, on the other hand, ensures the enjoyment of all the basic human rights by guaranteeing against any undue interference with the rights of the people either by the Legislature or by the Executive.

It is understandable why the draft Constitution created so much sensation among the people. Chistoshiyanaga observes: "Japan, like other Asian nations, has not in the past developed liberal traditions which the Western democracies take for granted as part of their political heritage. As a legacy of the long authoritarian tradition the populace still betray a fear of officials and there is a general reluctance on the part of individuals to challenge administrative actions or even question the wisdom of executive judgments. The bill of rights as contained in the new Constitution could, when understood and applied properly, go a long way toward rectifying the conditions and the psychology which stand in the way of democratization."[1]

Renunciation of War

Article 9 of the Constitution dealing with the "Renunciation of War" has been acclaimed as the most "dramatic provision"

[1] Chistoshiyanaga, *op. cit.*, p. 351.

of the Constitution though it has no direct impact on the fundamental issues—the sovereignty of the people, the structure of government, the relation of the people to their government, the issue of freedom and the pattern of political behaviour—and though the entire Article may be scrapped off the Constitution without affecting them in the least.

The Article reads as follows: "Aspiring sincerely to an international peace based on justice and order, the Japanese people renounce war as a sovereign right of the nation and the threat or use of force as means of settling international disputes.

"In order to accomplish the aim . . . land, sea and air forces, as well as other war potential, will never be maintained. The right of belligerency of the state will never be recognized."

This clear enunciation of pacifism has been described by Ardath Burks as the "unique and best known feature of the new Constitution." Dr. Takayanagi Kenzo interprets this Article as "a rhetorical political manifesto trumpeting pacifism".

That Article 9 of the Constitution was the product of American Occupation policy in Japan, there cannot be any doubt. The Supreme Commander of the Allied Powers (SCAP), General MacArthur, insisted that the new Constitution should renounce war and armed forces. In 1945-46 U.S. policy towards Japan was to dismantle her military structure and to cripple her permanently so that she would never have the potentialities to return to her policy during 1931 to 1945 and that the world would never be menaced by the aggressive designs of once a mighty military machine.

Johnstone has observed: "For Americans, the future of Japan is a special problem. This is true not only because the United States, as the greatest power in the Pacific, has a responsibility for leadership in the peace settlement, but also because the long history of conflicting policies between Japan and the United States has made the Japanese regard America as their number one enemy. An unreformed Japan is certain to be a menace to the general peace and security as well as a specific threat to the United States. American leadership can do much to insure the development of a reformed and peaceful Japan in the future and thus contribute to the security of all nations."[1]

[1] Johnstone, William C., *The Future of Japan*, p. 9.

On August 12, 1944, President Roosevelt stated in his radio address from the Puget Sound Navy Yard: "It is an unfortunate fact that other nations cannot trust Japan. It is an unfortunate fact that years of proof must pass before we can trust Japan and before we can classify Japan as a member of the society of nations which seeks permanent peace and whose word we can take."

As early as January 7, 1943, President Roosevelt stated in his message to Congress:

"It is clear to us that if Germany and Italy and Japan—or any one of them—remained armed at the end of this war or are permitted to rearm, they will again and inevitably embark upon an ambitious career of world conquest. They must be disarmed and kept disarmed."[1]

Ironically enough, this policy of disarmament and demilitarization was officially abandoned in 1951 by the U.S.-Japan Security Treaty. During this period power factors were at work to bring about a revision in the U.S. policy. "The problems and dangers of occupation policy are not very different from those which have arisen in Germany: demilitarisation has increasingly given way to the desire to preserve and rebuild Japan as a bulwark against Communism and Russia."[2]

Article 1 of the Japan-U.S. Security Treaty states: "Japan grants, and the United States of America accepts the right, upon the coming into force of the treaty of peace and of this treaty, to dispose United States land, air and sea forces in and about Japan. Such forces may be utilized to contribute to the maintenance of international peace and security in the Far East and to the security of Japan against armed attack from without, including assistance given at the express request of the Japanese Government to put down large scale internal riots and disturbances in Japan, caused by instigation or intervention by an outside power or powers."

However, Article 9 of the Constitution was welcomed by the great majority of the Japanese people. The reason is not far to seek. Japan was a defeated power and her people, terribly shocked by the horrors of war, were still smarting. Naturally, their desire for peace must be very sincere and genuine. They were eagerly looking for a world so ordered that relationship between

[1] Johnstone, *op. cit.*, p. 31.
[2] Friedmann, *An Introduction to World Politics*, p. 97.

nations shall become matters to be determined by cooperation and justice and not by aggression and military victory.

As Maki says: "The great majority of the people not only welcomed Article 9 from the time it first appeared, but also took great pride in it, then and later. They felt that it represented a complete rejection of the policies that had won Japan so much hatred and had brought disaster to the nation while it simultaneously opened the way to a peaceful future. Many also hoped that this thorough-going renunciation of war would be a good example to the rest of the world. Consequently it is little wonder that many Japanese have consistently defended Article 9 and have bitterly contested every governmental action that has seemed to undermine it."[1]

On the same Article observes Chistoshiyanaga: "Unprecedented was the incorporation of a provision for the renunciation of war as an instrument of national policy, a feature which was deemed by a not inconsiderable number of students of government, as somewhat visionary and unrealistic, if not actually utopian, in a world which has not succeeded in renouncing force in one form or another in international or even internal relations.[2]

"Nevertheless the Japanese people are undergoing an agonizing reappraisal, attempting to translate the statement of pacifist hopes into a program of security policy."[3]

It is now argued that Japan cannot permanently remain under the United States' nuclear umbrella. The geopolitical situation of Japan is such that she has two giant Communist states—the Soviet Union and the People's Republic of China—as her neighbours and she lives in close proximity to two other Communist states—North Korea and North Vietnam.

The people of Japan are really alarmed with Communist China's nuclear development. With the detonation of her thermonuclear bomb Japan is now constrained to think of reorienting her nuclear policy. Of course, in comparison to China, Japan is not lagging behind in nuclear development. But till now she is devoted to the application of nuclear energy to peaceful purposes.

[1] Maki, *op. cit.*, p. 83.   [2] Chistoshiyanaga, *op. cit.*, pp. 125-26.
[3] Burks, *op. cit.*, p. 263.

However, the grim realization of Japan's vulnerability to nuclear attack gives fresh and strong impetus to the mounting pressure for the development of nuclear energy for military purposes.

Koji Nakamura is of opinion that if militarism has not revived in Japan, it has never died either. Two statements, issued almost simultaneously by countries with opposing political systems, illustrate divergent assessments of Japan on the touchy issue of militarism.

One view comes from Chinese Premier Chou En-lai who declared, in a joint communique at the end of his North Korea visit, that militarism has firmly re-established itself in Japan, that the current U.S.-Japan Security Treaty is a military alliance designed against China and North Korea.

The other attitude is reflected in a report compiled by a commission from the U.S. House Foreign Affairs Committee which expressed concern over the emergence of a new militarism in Japan. The report says: "There seems to be a readiness to commit a substantial portion of Japan's vast wealth to the re-establishment of a major international military force. . . . This involves increased spending and much broader definition of her area of defence, nuclear capabilities and a clear determination to be a military power on a scale not contemplated since World War II."

Nakamura justifies this fear to a certain extent. "For, beneath the usual figures on the growing defence budget and expansion of defence areas, is the Japanese mentality: it is a rich fertile soil for the seeds of militarism to grow in and flourish from. This soil contains ingredients alien to outsiders. For one thing, the desire for a non-militarised Japan which underpinned General Douglas MacArthur's concept of a 'Switzerland of the Orient' has died aborning. As Japan's economy regained strength and living conditions improved partly due to the economic windfall from the Korean war, the memory of misery and defeat in World War II began to fade.

"The flame of pacifism also began flickering in the face of a growing, if subconscious, feeling that war itself was not wrong. What was wrong was the defeat. The guilt complex toward wrong committed during the war has also fast disappeared."

Nakamura attributes these feelings to Japanese nationalism. He says: "A society essentially feudal, both in structure and

and philosophy (the supreme value for man is devotion to his country), a society where the soil rejects individualism and liberal democracy absorbs totalitarianism and fascism."

He holds America partly responsible for the erosion of Japan's "feeble pacifism".

Incidentally it may be mentioned that Japan signed the Nuclear Non-Proliferation Treaty with definite reservations.

On the security problem of Japan in the decade of the 1970s, Vice-Foreign Minister Nobuhiko Ushiba wrote in the August 1969 edition of the monthly review *Sekaino Ugoki* (World Currents):

"Even following June, 1970, Japan's security will continue to be based upon its own defence capacity and the U.S.-Japan Security system which provides supplementary support. However, what we must bear in mind is that new significance should be given to this security system, which originally was a by-product of the cold war, and that in this process, we must keep under constant review the operations of the Security Treaty and the question of what Japan's defence capacity should be. Although the Security Treaty will continue as a deterrent against aggression, its functions will naturally change with the progress of time. But its most important significance, which will remain unchanged in the 1970s, is the fact that it symbolizes the close cooperation between Japan and the United States.

"The Japanese people, without losing sight of the importance of this cooperative relationship, must calmly and positively assess international situation and must cope with the problem of how they themselves should assume responsibility for the nation's security. This, then, must be the basic approach to the important issue of Japan's security in the coming decade of the 1970s."

The Vice-Foreign Minister regrets the sharp division of public opinion in Japan on this important issue and says:

"This is an abnormal state of affairs for a nation such as Japan which has the capacity of a world power. Although there may be many reasons for this strange situation, the greatest is the inexperience of the Japanese people in assessing the international situation which is a basic requisite in considering a nation's security."

CHAPTER 4

The Emperor

The day Japan surrenders, the United Nations must be prepared to decide upon the most fundamental problem of Japan's future: the postwar status of the Imperial Throne. This is not merely a question of the position of the present Emperor, Hirohito, and the Imperial family. It is the larger problem of an institution which has been the core of national beliefs, political system, and social structure of ceventy million people.

—William C. Johnstone

T H E C O N S T I T U T I O N of 1889, Japan's "modern Constitution", was a "gracious gift" from Emperor Meiji and not a product of the will of the people. Until 1947 it remained the fundamental law of the country. By its very nature, the Constitution was to have an authoritarian character. The Emperor was the source of all authority and omnipotent. All laws were to emanate from him, obedience to which was a sacred duty, the Emperor being "sacred and inviolable."

This will be clear from the three Articles of the Constitution:

Article I: The Empire of Japan shall be reigned over and governed by a line of Emperors unbroken for ages eternal.

Article III: The Emperor is sacred and inviolable.

Article IV: The Emperor is the head of the Empire, combining in Himself the rights of sovereignty, and exercises them according to the provisions of the present Constitution.

There was no democratic separation of powers under the Constitution. All powers were concentrated in a single source—the Emperor. The supreme and sovereign power of the Emperor comprised the fields of legislation, administration and judicature. And since it was physically impossible for the Emperor to exercise all these powers directly and personally,

23

powers had necessarily to be delegated to functionaries for their proper exercise. These functionaries acted as the agents of the Emperor and not in their individual responsibility or in any sense of responsibility to the people.

This will be clear from the observation of an eminent professor of Constitutional Law made in 1940: "The judicial power exercised by the Courts of justice in the name of the Tenno (Emperor), the executive power exercised by various administrative organs outside of matters personally attended to by the Tenno. and the legislative power exercised with the consent of the Imperial Diet—all merge in the supreme power of the Tenno, Although these powers are not personally wielded by the Tenno, the Courts of justice and the administrative organs possess their respective rights as entrusted to them by the Tenno, so that, it may be said, they all emanate from the supreme power of the Tenno. As to the exercise of legislative power, the consent of the Imperial Diet is needed, which consent means only that the Diet gives its consent to the legislative act of the Tenno and nothing more. The Tenno exercises it personally over His Subjects."

The Constitution gives the Emperor, the supreme command of the Army and Navy, the power to declare war, to make peace and to conclude treaties. It empowers him to make emergency legislation. The Constitution also gives the Emperor the power to initiate projects to amend the provisions of the Constitution.

But this is only the legal and constitutional position of the Emperor. Never were the "modern" Emperors of Japan allowed to exercise their constitutional powers. The Emperor remained always the source of all authority but this authority was exercised by "the real rulers of Japan—the militarists bureaucrats, politicians, nobility and industrial monopolists". As Johnstone has observed: "There is no evidence that any Emperor under the Constitution has exercised more than an evanescent influence over affairs of state. Rather, the real bosses of Japan bend the Emperor to their will, for he is part and parcel of the autocratic, controlled society they have created, and the Throne is the hub around which their totalitarian system revolves."[1]

[1] Johnstone, William C., *The Future of Japan*, pp. 88-9.

The principle of the British constitutional democracy that the King reigns but does not rule applies to the Emperor of Japan. He has reigned but seldom ruled.

A dramatic incident that took place on September 6, 1940, reveals the helpless, unenviable position of the Emperor. Emperor Hirohito convened a meeting of Japan's leaders who gathered round a long rectangular table in the No. 1 East Room of the Imperial Palace with the Emperor on a dais at the head. As the Prime Minister Fumimaro Konoye began to read "Outline Plan for National Policy", the Emperor sat motionless and seemingly impassive, shedding his "divine radiance."

The Prime Minister disclosed that "the empire was determined to risk war with the United States, Britain and the Netherlands to achieve its economic ends, and war preparations were to be completed by late October". Most of the leaders present at the occasion echoed the Prime Minister and unanimously agreed to start hostilities immediately with the United States. They missed their "finest hour" when France fell and they should not miss it a second time when the Russians were collapsing before the invading Germans.

Suddenly, to everybody's astonishment, the Emperor rose to speak, which he never did. With all the members of the Conference hardly daring to breathe, Hirohito began to read the poem "The Four Sides of the Sea" written by his grandfather, Emperor Meiji, in a mood of high seriousness:

I think all the people of the world are brethren.
Then why are the waves and winds so unsettled today.

The Emperor pleaded for the realization of his grandfather's ideal of international peace. But the Chief of the Naval General Staff replied that they advocated war only as a last resort. The Emperor, however, was far from convinced. But since the leaders were unanimous in favour of war, the Emperor remained silent.

Churchill wrote in his *War Memoirs:* "The Emperor and the Imperial Princes, around whom gathered the highest aristocracy, were against an aggressive war. They had too much to lose in a violent era. Many of them had travelled and met their equals in foreign courts. They admired the life of Europe

and feared its power and that of the United States. They admired the secure majesty of the English monarchy. They leaned
continuously upon their skin-deep parliamentarianism, and
hoped they might continue to reign or rule in peace. But who
should say what the Army would do? No patriarchate, no
Emperor, no dynasty could separate themselves from it. The
Emperor and the Princes were for peace and prudence, but
had no wish to perish for such a cause."[1]

Those who believe that Emperor Hirohito could have stop-
ped the war in 1941, had he wished, do not understand his
subtle and complex position. Like the King of England he
could advise, warn or encourage but certainly not prevent.

"He could only counsel—and ratify. For the Emperor must
be at one with his government to preserve the monolithic unity
of the nation. He was lashed to the mast of his own boundless
prestige."[2]

"Thus, whether we choose to regard the modern Japanese
emperor as puppets, partial puppets or even active political
participants in the affairs of state, the institution has shown itself
unable to check the course of Japanese political and military
aggression. On the contrary, the Emperor institution in the
hands of several generations of Japanese statesmen and bureaucrats, variously described as liberal, moderate or reactionary,
has been the chosen instrument to indoctrinate the people with
a racism as malignant as Nazism, with an unscientific tribal
exclusiveness and with a contempt for human life whether
Japanese or foreign that has nothing in common with the quali-
ties of courage or sacrifice since it is nourished by an inhuman
and anti-social fanaticism. This institution has invariably ser-
ved as the magic charm, which in the hands of those who
have guided Japanese policy for the past fifty years, has dazzled,
beguiled and finally debauched the minds of all but the most
heroically humane and intelligent Japanese."[3]

However, Emperor Hirohito is reported to have told General
MacArthur that he was ready "to bear sole responsibility for

---

[1] Churchill, *War Memoirs*, Vol. II, p. 458.
[2] From the summary of the book *Tora, Tora, Tora!* by Dr. Gordon Prange,
published in Readers Digest, January, 1964.
[3] "A Canadian View", *Pacific Affairs*, June 1944.

every political and military decision made and action taken by my people in the conduct of the war". Nevertheless, the Emperor was not indicted as a war criminal. The Americans did not like to submit the Throne to indignities. Rather they decided to use it as a basis of control and democratization.

Why the Emperor?

It was the destiny of Japan to have a Constitution tailored to her by her erstwhile enemy, the United States. But it could not possibly be a Japanese version of the American Constitution although American influence is obvious and apparent. Conditions must be created to make the Constitution look like Japanese. In other words, the Constitution must be acceptable to the Japanese people.

But, how could a Constitution be accepted by the people of Japan—whose first act of the day was to bow in reverence in the direction of the Imperial Palace (this pre-war tradition is, of course, not observed today)—without their Emperor?

"The Emperor has been and still is the living symbol of the nation's history, heritage, and achievements, of all that is glorious in the nation's past and present, of its continuity and durability. He is the incarnation of history and religion. In his person are epitomized the nation's hopes, aspirations, and promise."[1]

The Japanese people revere their Emperor in an emotional and religious spirit the only comparison of which can be found in the British people who derive from the Throne a "sense of anchorage and stability", a sense that "whatever the future may bring it will not break too radically with the tried and proven concepts of the past."[2]

In pre-war Japan schoolchildren were taught: "We subjects who live under such an illustrious Imperial family are for the most part descendants of the gods .... It is clear that the foundation of our state has been superior from ancient times to that of other countries."

The Vice-Speaker of the elected House of Representatives could say:

[1] Yanaga, Chitoshi, *Japanese People and Politics*, p. 129.
[2] Neumann, R. G., *European and Comparative Governments*.

"The Emperor is to the Japanese mind the Supreme being in the cosmos of Japan as god is in the universe of the pantheistic philosopher. From Him everything emanates, in Him everything subsists; there is nothing on the soil of Japan existent independent of Him. He is the sole owner of the Empire, the author of law, justice, privilege and honour, and the symbol of the unity of the Japanese nation. He needs no Pope or archbishop to crown Him at His accession. He is supreme in all temporal matters and He is the foundation of Japanese social and civil morality."

And a Premier (Prince Konoye) could safely state:

"Our movement must not stop at the creation of a mutual co-prosperity sphere in East Asia alone. We must prosecute the movement for all time and so realize peace and security for the whole world. . . . The movement is based on the spirit of the Imperial way. In short, the basic objective for which the movement is being conducted is for the assistance to the Throne."

These indicate the traditional and emotional attachment of the people to the Emperor and his family. It must be clear, therefore, that an institution, which had been in existence for centuries drawing the affection of the people and their family feeling, enjoying their unalloyed obedience and respect, could not possibly have been eliminated by a single stroke without taking the risk of violent revolution.

Moreover, Emperor Hirohito was very much helpful to the Allies in bringing World War II to end. Millions of Japan's troops laid down their arms in obedience to the Imperial Rescript of Surrender, September 1-2, 1945. Incidentally, it may be referred here that first Japanese offer of surrender, August 10, 1945, made it a condition that Potsdam Proclamation "did not include any demand for a change in the status of the Emperor under the national laws."

The logic of the situation, therefore, prompted the United States and the Allies (Soviet Union, however, was opposed to the retention of the Throne) not to make the Emperor "an immediate target of their vengeance", but to retain the Imperial Throne as "an element of stability in Japan to avoid the revolution which they fear should the Emperor be deposed and the

Throne eliminated." "His mere presence on the Throne gave the people a sense of continuity that helped them go through the upheaval of transition from one system to another with a minimum of disorder."[1]

Further, it must be remembered also that although the Constitution of 1889 gave the Emperor absolute powers, never once had the Emperor any occasion to exercise them on his own. He was passive and a "tool", so to say, used by the extremists and the militarists to satisfy their aggressive designs and to perpetuate a feudal, militaristic society. If this be so, there is no reason why the same "tool" could not be used as a base by the moderates and the pacifists for a liberal, democratic and peaceful development.

Quigley and Turner, therefore, observe: "Appreciation of the profound significance of the Imperial house in Japanese political life led the Allies to permit its survival as a political institution."[2]

On the other hand, those who opposed the retention of the Throne argued that if Emperor Hirohito was to be spared because he was powerless to check the course of Japan's political and military aggression, what will be the value of the Imperial Rescript for the introduction of democracy by the Will of Heaven? If the Emperor was really innocent but nevertheless so powerful a force that he must be kept and used, then why was he not able to rally the better elements among his people and to prevent a disastrous war? Either he is a puppet and, therefore, useless for the purposes of democracy or he is powerful and should have checked the adventurists. "He cannot be both. Either way he is a malevolent factor . . . . Democracy by Imperial Rescript would be nothing less than a continuation of the Japanese game of hoodwinking the world . . . . There is no short-cut to democracy. Democracy lies in the will of the people to rule themselves. Its source cannot be the will of a Mikado, whether or not he is thought to be a god."[3]

Further, there was the consideration that "it would be unjust and illogical to spare the Emperor and punish other elements responsible for war."

[1] Maki, John M., *Government and Politics in Japan*, p. 64.
[2] Harold S. Quigley and John E. Turner, *The New Japan*, p. 5.
[3] "The Mikado Must Go" by Dr. Sun Fo. *Foreign Affairs*, October, 1944.

But the Government of the United States could not ignore the sentiment of the people. It was correctly understood that the indictment of the Emperor as war criminal and the abolition of the Throne would make the Emperor a martyr in the eyes of the people. It would have intensified their hatred against the United States and rendered the construction of a new governmental system impossible. As Johnstone has observed: "The Japanese people might regard the abolition of the Throne as such an unwarranted and unnecessary attack upon their most sacred national institution that they would refuse to co-operate with any liberal groups who wished to take advantage of the United Nations assistance in the trying tasks of political, economic and social reform. If this occurred, the United Nations would face the problem of either continuing to occupy and administer Japan indefinitely or of modifying the original policy. Or, if a new government was formed, many Japanese might regard such a regime as a puppet of the United Nations, and their compatriots in such a government as 'collaborators' with their enemies. The United Nations would then be in a position of supporting a government that lacked inherent stability and would collapse as soon as their support was withdrawn."[1]

The advantages of the retention of the Throne thus seem to outweigh the disadvantages. So long as the Emperor is there no other individual can capture completely "the loyalty and adoration of the people as dictators have done elsewhere."[2]

The Emperor Under the New Constitution

To any casual reader of Japanese social and political history, it must be clear that the Emperor and his family was no part of Japanese life. The Emperor was a god on earth, an object of awe and veneration and, therefore, "different" from the millions of his "Subjects".

The Emperor "ascended the Throne of a lineal succession unbroken for ages eternal". He is "supreme being in the cosmos of Japan as god is in the universe of the pantheistic philosopher. From Him everything emanates, in Him everything subsists; there is nothing on the soil of Japan existent independent of

[1] Johnstone, *op. cit.*, p. 95.
[2] McNelly, Theodore, *Contemporary Government of Japan*, p. 68.

Him. He is the sole owner of the Empire, the author of law, justice and honour, and the symbol of the unity of the Japanese nation. He needs no Pope or archbishop to crown Him at His accession. He is supreme in all temporal matters and He is the foundation of Japanese social and civil morality."

Thus was created the myth of divinity of the Emperor.

The new Constitution destroys this myth and marks the beginning of a new role for the Emperor in Japanese society. No longer shall the Emperor live in high pedestals of divinity, in lofty detachment from the people. No longer shall he have any halo about him. The people from now on shall have the comfortable feeling that the Emperor is one among them and one with them.

Curiously enough Emperor Hirohito himself took the initiative towards the humanization of the Imperial Institution. On January 1, 1946, the Emperor made a startling declaration to he people:

"The ties between us and our people have always stood upon mutual trust and affection. They do not depend upon mere legends and myths. They are not predicated on the false conception that the Emperor is divine and the Japanese people are superior to other races and fated to rule the world."[1]

The people, naturally, were not prepared for such a declaration. So there was stir and surprise all round. But the people felt comfortable at the idea that henceforth the Emperor was to be close to them. Emperor Hirohito initiated a long series of public appearances in civilian clothes in places formerly thought unfit for imperial presence. Thus, in outward appearance too, the Emperor was to be no different from the people. He visited mines, factories and farms, attended baseball games and even a movie. "It was a novel experience for the people to meet their ruler face to face, which they had never done before, but they liked it."[2]

Under the new Constitution, the Emperor like the British monarch shall reign but shall not rule. Article 1 of the Constitution says: "The Emperor shall be the symbol of the state and of the unity of the people, deriving his position from the will of the people with whom resides sovereign power." The obvious

---

[1] Maki, *op. cit.*, pp. 66-7.   [2] Yanaga, *op. cit.*, p. 139.

implication of this Article is that the institution of the Emperor can be abolished if the people so desire.

Under the old Constitution, theoretically the Emperor was the source of all powers—executive, legislative and judicial. But the new Constitution gives him no governmental power. He is only to be a symbol. Article 4 of the Constitution says:

"The Emperor shall perform only such acts in matters of state as may be provided in this Constitution and he shall not have powers related to Government."

Theoretically the British Queen is still the source of all powers. In practice, however, such powers are exercised by the Cabinet in the name of the Queen. And the entire responsibility for administration is borne by the Cabinet. But, if the Queen suddenly decides to act on her own, disregarding the ministerial advice, legally there is nothing to resist her. Of course, during the last two hundred years, no British monarch took such a decision. But the point is, there is no constitutional bar. Whatever restrictions there may be, they are not legal or constitutional, but political.

The position of the Emperor, on the other hand, is constitutionally registered. Article 3 of the Constitution says:

"The advice and approval of the Cabinet shall be required for all acts of the Emperor in matters of state, and the Cabinet shall be responsible therefor."

Thus, what is a matter of practice and convention in Great Britain, is a matter of Constitutional Law in Japan.

The critics of the new Constitution assert that the symbolic status of the Emperor, popular sovereignty and denial of even nominal powers of the government to the Emperor indicate that Japan is not a constitutional monarchy but a republic. But, as Quigley and Turner point out, Article 4 of the Constitution which clumsily states that the Emperor "shall not have powers related to government" is "contradicted by others that authorize the Emperor to appoint the prime minister and the chief judge of the Supreme Court, to promulgate laws and orders, to convoke the Diet and dissolve the House of Representatives, etc. All such acts are exercises of governmental power, whether or not they are done upon "advice and approval" of the Cabinet."[1]

[1] Quigley and Turner, *op. cit.*, p. 202.

In Great Britain, however, the convention that the monarch acts on the advice of the Cabinet applies not only in matters of state but even in extremely private and personal matters. This was exemplified in the abdication crisis of 1936. The religion of the King has been restricted since the 17th century. (The British monarch must be a Protestant. No Roman Catholic can be the King or Queen of England.) The abdication crisis revealed that the Parliament through the Prime Minister could even control King's choice of a wife.

The rule that the King must act on the advice of the Cabinet applies even to the members of the royal family. Margaret's love affair, her marriage and the furore created over a very casual observation of Prince Philip on the policy of the British Government towards Rhodesia bear ample testimony to this. But the Japanese Emperor shall be bound by the advice and approval of the Cabinet in matters of state. The Cabinet advice and approval does not relate to his personal and private matters. Nor are the members of his family involved in this.

The British Constitution offers two unique opportunities to the Queen to act on her own. One is the choice of the Prime Minister and the other, the dissolution of Parliament. Normally of course, the Queen shall have no choice in the appointment of the Prime Minister. Following the parliamentary practice the Queen appoints the leader of the majority party in the House of Commons as the Prime Minister. But at times she may have a real choice. The appointment of Lord Hume as the Prime Minister of Great Britain proved this beyond doubt.

Lord Hume was not the leader of the Conservative majority in the House of Commons. Nor was he a member of that House. It was observed in some quarters that the Queen acted on the advice of the outgoing Prime Minister Macmillan. But it must be remembered that the British constitutional practice does not bind the Queen with the advice of an outgoing Prime Minister. Therefore, the choice of Lord Hume as the Prime Minister of Great Britain may be interpreted as her own choice. To quote Munro: "During the brief interval between the resignation of one Prime Minister and the installation of another, the King is the sole depository of executive power."

But the Japanese Constitution will not permit the Emperor to have any choice in the appointment of the Prime Minister.

Article 6 of the Constitution clearly says: "The Emperor shall appoint the Prime Minister as designated by the Diet."

Again, under normal circumstances the Queen acts on the question of the dissolution of the House of Commons on the advice of the Prime Minister. But this does not mean that the Prime Minister can always have a dissolution of the House of Commons. There are occasions when the Queen may refuse a dissolution. On this point Lord Asquith has said: "The dissolution of Parliament is in this country one of the prerogatives of Crown . . . . It does not mean that the Crown should act arbitrarily and without the advice of the responsible Ministers, but it does mean that the Crown is not bound to take the advice of a particular Minister to put its subjects to the tumult and turmoil of a series of General Elections so long as it can find other Ministers who are prepared to give contrary advice."

Here also, it will be seen that the Emperor is in an unenviable position. Article 7 of the Constitution lists the acts which the Emperor shall perform "with the advice and approval of the Cabinet". Dissolution of the House of Representatives (Lower House of the Diet) is included in this list. The plain meaning is this, if the Emperor is advised by the Cabinet to dissolve the House of Representatives, he cannot refuse. As Chitoshi Yanaga observes: "He does not call a party leader to form a government, he simply performs the ceremony of appointing a Prime Minister who has already been formally selected by the Diet. He has no power to refuse a dissolution of the Diet such as the British monarch enjoys as a prerogative."[1]

Again, under the new Constitution "The Prime Minister shall appoint the Ministers of State . . . . The Prime Minister may remove the Ministers of State as he chooses."[1] Thus, regarding the appointment and removal of Ministers of State, the Emperor shall have nothing to do. Under the British Constitution such appointments and removals take place through the Queen, although normally she has no choice in the matter. But in Great Britain every Minister including the Prime Minister is a Minister of Her Majesty's Government.

Moreover, the English constitutional government allows the Queen to be informed of all the affairs of the state. Queen

[1] Yanaga, *op. cit.*, p. 141   [2] Art. 68.

Victoria always insisted that nothing should be done without her knowledge. The Emperor, however, shall have no claim to be informed of what is going on. It all depends on the Ministers whether to keep the Emperor informed or not.

Article 74 of the new Constitution says: "All laws and Cabinet orders shall be signed by the competent Minister of State and countersigned by the Prime Minister." Thus, for the laws to be effective, assent of the Emperor is not necessary.

In Great Britain, on the other hand, no Bill can be a law without the assent of the Queen and (theoretically at least) the Queen may refuse assent.

From these, it must be clear that the Emperor compared with the British monarch will have a very insignificant role in the governmental process. Whatever influence he may bring to bear on the government, it must be moral.

The new Constitution brings about changes in the economic position of the İmperial House. Under the old Constitution the Imperial House and the finances were outside the control of the government. Now, they have been brought under the control of the Diet. Article 8 of the Constitution says: "No property can be given to, or received by, the Imperial House, nor can any gifts be made therefrom, without the authorization of the Diet."

The Constitution, however, confirms: "The Imperial Throne shall be dynastic and succeeded to in accordance with the Imperial House Law passed by the Diet."[1]

The Constitution also provides for regency. "When in accordance with the Imperial House Law, a regency is established the Regent shall perform his acts in matters of state in the Emperor's name."[2]

The Emperor, however, shall perform certain ceremonial functions on behalf of the people and with the advice and approval of the Cabinet. These are:

Promulgation of amendments of the Constitution, laws, Cabinet orders and treaties, convocation of the Diet.

Dissolution of the House of Representatives. Proclamation of general election of members of the Diet.

[1] Art. 2.   [2] Art. 5.

Attestation of the appointment and dismissal of Ministers of State and other officials as provided for by law, and of full powers and credentials of Ambassadors and Ministers.

Attestation of general and special amnesty, commutation of punishment, reprieve, and restoration of rights.

Awarding of honours.

Attestation of instruments of ratification and other diplomatic documents as provided for by law.

Receiving foreign Ambassadors and Ministers.

Performance of ceremonial functions.[1]

The actual functions of the Emperor are substantially what they were before the promulgation of the new Constitution.

In conclusion, it may be said that the Emperor like the British monarch "is the object of the adulation of the people". In 1911-12, when Emperor Meiji was dangerously ill, the people in thousands anxiously waited outside the Imperial House, praying for the recovery of the Emperor. A similar attitude was displayed by the British people in 1929 when King George V fell seriously ill. The enthusiasm and interest of the people in the royal family found eloquent expressions on several occasions thereafter—when Crown Prince Akihito was born in 1933 and then again in his marriage ceremony. Dr. Yanaga observes: "The reverence for the Emperor is almost unbelievable especially to those who have not witnessed its manifestation at first hand. Furthermore, it is unfathomable since it is an emotional and practically a religious manifestation. Perhaps the British alone of the Western peoples today can come closest to understanding the Japanese attitude toward the sovereign."[2]

[1] Art. 7.
[2] Yanaga, *op. cit.*, p. 130.

CHAPTER 5
The Cabinet

Today the parliamentary system, on the British pattern, is the central feature of the Japanese government.

—Quigley and Turner

T H E O L D Constitution of the Empire of Japan did not make any provision for Cabinet. Cabinet in Japan was extra-constitutional as it is in the United States and Great Britain. The words "Cabinet" and "Prime Minister" were not to be found in the Meiji Constitution.

Cabinet was initiated in 1885 in anticipation of the promulgation of the Imperial Constitution in 1889 by an Imperial Ordinance which created nine (9) administrative departments which became the Cabinet. Thus, the Cabinet as an institution antedated the promulgation of the Constitution by four (4) years. The development of the Cabinet in Great Britain is thus found to be reversed in Japan. In Great Britain the evolution of the system of parliamentary government was completed by the addition of the Cabinet to its other three elements: the electorate, the political parties and the Parliament.

There was, under the old Constitution, a Cabinet but not the Cabinet system. Chapter IV of the Constitution deals with "the Ministers of State and the Privy Council". Article 55 of the Chapter says: "The respective Ministers of State shall give their advice to the Emperor, and be responsible for it.

"All laws, Imperial Ordinances and Imperial Rescripts' of whatever kind, that relate to the affairs of the state, require the counter-signature of a Minister of State."

But the Ministers of State never worked as a team. There was a Prime Minister but the Ministers of State were not under his leadership. There were so many individual Ministers of State and they advised the Emperor individually and separately. The Prime Minister was only the "moderator of a group of equals".

Political homogeneity of the Ministers and the leadership of the Prime Minister are the two recognized principles of the British Cabinet system of government. Another principle of Cabinet government is the collective responsibility of the Ministers to the representatives of the people in the legislature and through them to the nation.

Under the Meiji Constitution the Ministers of State were responsible to the Emperor, and since the Emperor was merely a symbol of power they were "in practice responsible to themselves or to the oligarchy which ruled from behind the Emperor. "The Ministers were not responsible to the Diet nor were they obliged to resign upon a vote of no confidence by the Diet."

Moreover, in a Cabinet government, Cabinet is the chief executive head of the government and bears full responsibility for every branch of administration and exercises authority in its own right. Under the Constitution of 1889, however, executive power belonged to the Emperor and he determined "the organization of the different branches of administration." The Ministers of State exercised such powers as were delegated to them by the Emperor.

Chitoshi Yanaga has referred to several other factors responsible for the "weakness of the Cabinet under the old system." These were the Privy Council which "proved to be the bane of existence for the Prime Minister", the House of Peers which "did not hesitate to make the effective functioning of the Cabinet impossible," and the army which had the power to make or break the Cabinet, and finally "the degeneration of Cabinet Ministers into mere administrative heads of departments."[1]

Added to these was the multiplicity of political parties which made the overthrow of a government very easy. This is clear from the fact that during the period from 1885 to 1945 forty-one (41) Cabinets were formed.

The new Constitution of Japan, however, accepts all the principles of the British parliamentary system of government.

[1] Yanaga, Chitoshi, *Japanese People and Politics*, p. 145.

It gives the executive power to the Cabinet, makes it the director of national affairs. The leadership of the Prime Minister is recognized and the Cabinet is made collectively responsible to the Diet and to the nation. This will be clear from the following provisions of the Constitution:

Article 65 : Executive power shall be vested in the Cabinet.

Article 66 : The Cabinet shall consist of the Prime Minister, who shall be its head, and other Ministers of State, as provided for by law.

The Cabinet, in the exercise of executive power, shall be collectively responsible to the Diet.

Article 69 : If the House of Representatives passes a no-confidence resolution or rejects a confidence resolution, the Cabinet shall resign en masse, unless the House of Representatives is dissolved within ten (10) days.

Thus, the collective responsibility of the British Cabinet, which means that the Cabinet shall rise and fall as a team and that it remains in office so long as it commands the confidence of the majority in the House of Commons and goes out the moment it forfeits such confidence, has been registered in the Constitution. "In other words, powers which were (under the Meiji Constitution) assigned to an amorphous executive, appointed in the name of, and responsible solely to the, Emperor, have now been shifted to the Cabinet."[1]

Quigley and Turner observe: "Joint or collective responsibility for Cabinet decisions, individual responsibility for those within the jurisdiction of the Ministry involved, constitute the basic rules of Cabinet action, modelled upon those of the United Kingdom."[2]

Again, as in Great Britain, secrecy of the Cabinet proceedings is rigidly maintained by regulations.

In Japan, however, all the Ministers (even those without portfolio) are Cabinet Ministers and they attend Cabinet meetings in their own rights. Prime Minister's note of request is not necessary for the purpose. In Great Britain, on the other hand, only the Cabinet Ministers (that is, Ministers who hold important portfolios) attend Cabinet meetings and make policy

[1] Burks Ardath W., *The Government of Japan*, p. 105.
[2] Quigley and Turner, *The New Japan*, p. 195.

decisions. Others may attend but only on a note of request form the Prime Minister.

Yet, on another point, Cabinet system in Japan differs from that in Great Britain. Whereas in Great Britain Cabinet decides by majority, in Japan Cabinet decisions must always be unanimous. Since the Cabinet is collectively responsible to the Diet unanimity must be secured and if a Minister fails to agree with the Cabinet decision he must resign or else he may be summarily dismissed by the Prime Minister.

Composition of the Cabinet

The Cabinet under the new Japanese Constitution consists of the Prime Minister who is its head and other Ministers of State as provided for by law.[1] Law provides that the Cabinet shall be composed of the Prime Minister and eighteen Ministers of State.[2] Article 3 (2) of the Cabinet Law provides for "appointment of Ministers who have no specific share of administrative affairs under their charge".

At present there are twelve (12) administrative departments each in charge of a Minister. There are also four (4) Ministers without portfolio.

The Cabinet consists of the following Ministries besides the office of the Prime Minister and Board of Audit: Ministry of Justice, Ministry of Foreign Affairs, Ministry of Finance, Ministry of Education, Ministry of Health and Welfare, Ministry of Agriculture and Forestry, Ministry of International Trade and Industry, Ministry of Transport, Ministry of Post and Telecommunications, Ministry of Labour, Ministry of Construction and the Ministry of Home Affairs.

Besides these Ministries the national government organization necessary for the efficient prosecution of national administrative affairs includes the following Commissions and Agencies:

Commissions: Fair Trade Commission, National Public Safety Commission, Land Coordination Commission, National Capital Region Development Commission, Administrative Commission of National Bar Examination, Public Safety Investigation

---

[1] Art. 66.   [2] Art. 2 of the Cabinet Law.

Commission, Central Labour Relations Commission, Public Corporation and National Enterprise Labour Relations Commission.

Agencies: Imperial Household Agency, Administrative Management Agency, Hokkaido Development Agency, Defence Agency, Economic Planning Agency, Science and Technology Agency, Defence Facilities Administration Agency, Public Security Investigation Agency, Tax Administration Agency, Culture Affairs Agency, Social Insurance Agency, Food Agency, Forestry Agency, Fisheries Agency, Patent Office Smaller Enterprises Agency, Maritime Safety Agency, Marine Accidents Inquiry Agency, Meteorological Agency, Fire Defence Agency.

National Government Organization Law permits each Ministry to have one Parliamentary Vice-Minister. Ministry of Finance, Ministry of Agriculture and Forestry, Ministry of International Trade and Industry, however, are allowed to have two Parliamentary Vice-Ministers each. The function of the Vice-Minister is to "assist the Minister heading the Ministry or Agency, participate in the formation of policies and in programme planning, conduct the political affairs; and, under prior orders of the Minister heading the Ministry or Agency, perform the Minister's functions on his behalf in the absence of the Minister."[1]

The national government organs are under the control and jurisdiction of the Cabinet. They have well defined scope of authority and responsibility and maintain liaison with one another so that they may consummate their administrative functions as an organic whole. The Prime Minister decides on any point of doubt relating to the jurisdiction between competent Ministers.

The Constitution provides that the majority of the members of the Cabinet must be chosen from among the members of the Diet.[2] It is thus constitutionally possible to appoint a fewer than half of the members of the Cabinet from outside the Diet. But the tendency is to appoint the Ministers from among the membership of the Diet.

The Japanese practice, therefore, is in tune with the British Convention which demands the Ministers to be members of

---

[1] Art. 17 (3) of *National Government Organization Law*.   [2] Art. 68.

either House of Parliament. A non-member may be appointed a Minister but he must become a member of Parliament through election or nomination at a subsequent date failing which he forfeits his position in the Ministry.

Functions of the Cabinet

Article 65 of the Constitution vests in the Cabinet the executive power. However, executive power is not defined by the Constitution or by Cabinet law. It is to be understood, therefore, that the Cabinet will perform all the administrative functions which comprise the executive power. Burks observes: "Clearly such power is not vested in the Crown to be exercised by the Cabinet, as in England. Nor has the power of the Cabinet grown in an entirely extra-constitutional fashion, as in the United States."[1]

Article 73 of the Constitution says:

The Cabinet, in addition to other general administrative functions, shall perform the following functions:

Administer the law faithfully; conduct affairs of state.

Manage foreign affairs.

Conclude treaties with the prior or subsequent approval of the Diet.

Administer the civil service, in accordance with standards established by law.

Prepare the budget and present it to the Diet.

Enact Cabinet orders in order to execute the provisions of the Constitution.

Decide on general amnesty, special amnesty, commutation of punishment, reprieve, and restoration of rights.

It is to be noted here that the functions of the Cabinet relating to amnesty, commutation of punishment, reprieve, etc., are in the nature of judicial powers and are the prerogatives of the executive head of the state such as the Queen of England and the President of India. In Japan, however, they become the prerogatives of the Cabinet.

In addition to the executive functions listed above the Cabinet performs other important functions which are connected with other organs of government.

[1] Burks, *op. cit.*, p. 107.

The Cabinet advises the Emperor in matters of state. According to Quigley and Turner, this is the most significant function of the Cabinet "since advice is equivalent to decision on his behalf, subject to such consideration of his views as is consonant with constitutional monarch".[1]

The Cabinet designates the Chief Judge of the Supreme Court. It appoints all judges of the Supreme Court except the Chief Judge and also the judges of the inferior courts.

Functions of the Cabinet connected with the Diet include the convocation of extraordinary session of the Diet and when the House of Representatives is dissolved, convocation of the House of Councillors in emergency session in time of national emergency.

It must be remembered, however, that the principal function of the Cabinet in Japan is legislative as much as it is in Great Britain. Constitutionally, the Diet is the highest organ of state power and the sole law-making organ of the state. But initiative in legislation belongs to the Cabinet. Under Article 72 of the Constitution the Prime Minister submits Bills, reports on general national affairs and foreign relations to the Diet. Article 5 of the Cabinet Law also provides the same thing. It says: "The Prime Minister, representing the Cabinet, shall submit Cabinet Bills, budgets and other proposals to the Diet, and shall report on general national affairs and foreign relations to the Diet."

As a matter of fact, legislators in Japan suffer from the same lack of technical knowledge as their counterparts in Great Britain which compel them to delegate legislative powers to the executive. Not only that most of the Bills adopted by the Diet are initiated by the Cabinet, they are also drafted by the public officials in general terms and are implemented by the executive orders so technical in nature that their comprehension requires an experienced lawyer. As Burks has observed: "Coupled with its legislative leadership is the fact that statutes are supplemented and executed by Cabinet orders so complex as to defy understanding by the ordinary legislature."[2]

Another powerful weapon at the armoury of the Cabinet to influence the course of legislation is the preparation of the bud-

[1] Quigley and Turner, *op. cit.*, p. 205.　　[2] Burks, *op. cit.*, pp. 107-08

get. Thus executive leadership in legislation is as much a fact in Japan as it is in Great Britain and in the United States. Chitoshi Yanaga has observed: "It is quite clear by now that the executive power in practice, if not in theory, plays a decisive role in legislation by making a political decision as to what policies are to be adopted and how they are to be formulated so that they will be acceptable and feasible as legislation."[1]

Referring to the spectacular rise of the Cabinet under the new Constitution from its humble position under the Meiji Constitution Quigley and Turner observe that it recalls the Biblical prophecy that "the last shall be first".

The Prime Minister

If the position of the British Prime Minister is one of exceptional authority then no less is that of the Prime Minister of Japan. The difference, however, is that while the position of the Japanese Prime Minister is constitutionally registered that of the Prime Minister of Great Britain is based mostly on conventions.

Like the Prime Minister of Great Britain he is the supreme political leader of the nation and the constitutional head of government. He owes his political position to his being the directly elected representative of the people and his being the leader of the strongest and majority party in the Diet.

Under the old Constitution of Japan the Prime Minister was no more than first among equals. But the new Constitution stipulates his position in clear and unambiguous terms: "The Cabinet shall consist of the Prime Minister, who shall be its head, and other Ministers of State, as provided for by law."[2] Incidentally, it may be noted here that it was the policy of the Occupation Government to enhance the position and prestige of the Prime Minister and General MacArthur did everything in this direction.

As the head of the Cabinet, the Prime Minister presides over Cabinet meetings and in his absence, the Vice-Premier. The Vice-Premier is the spokesman of the Prime Minister, "a liaison

[1] Yanaga, *op. cit.*, p. 149.   [2] Art. 66.

man in the Cabinet, and a powerful voice in policy-making. With a position somewhat analogous to that of the Vice-President of the United States, the deputy has come to occupy a position of even greater prestige and influence."[1]

The Prime Minister exercises control and supervision over various administrative branches, submits Cabinet Bills, budgets and other proposals to the Diet and reports on general national affairs and foreign relations to it.

The superiority of the Prime Minister over other Ministers of State is further emphasized by the constitutional requirement that all laws and Cabinet orders signed by the competent Ministers of State must have to be countersigned by the Prime Minister;[2] by his legal authority to "suspend the offiicial act or order of any administration office, pending action by the Cabinet,"[3] by his authority to decide on any point of doubt relating to jurisdiction as between the competent Ministers."[4]

The most important power of the Prime Minister, however, is his unquestioned authority to appoint and dismiss the Ministers of State. The Constitution says: "The Prime Minister shall appoint the Ministers of State. The Prime Minister may remove the Ministers of State as he chooses."[5]

In fact, his hand is as much free or as much restricted as that of the British Prime Minister in matters of appointment. His choice is influenced by party considerations and several other factors. Like the Prime Minister of England, he "must strive to make his Cabinet as broadly representative as possible—having regard to sectional, social, religious and economic affiliations."[6]

The power of the Prime Minister to "remove the Ministers of State as he chooses" was demonstrated first in November, 1947, by the dismissal of Agriculture and Forestry Minister Hirano by Prime Minister Katayama and again in March, 1953, by Prime Minister Yoshida who removed Agriculture and Forestry Minister Hirokawa.

The Constitution strengthens the hand of the Prime Minister yet in another way. It provides: "When there is a vacancy in

---

[1] Burks, *op. cit.*, p. 107. [2] Art. 74.
[3] Art. 8 of the Cabinet Law. [4] Art. 7 of the Cabinet Law.
[5] Art. 68. [6] Munro.

the post of Prime Minister...the Cabinet shall resign en masse."[1] Thus, the Prime Minister may always hold out the threat of resignation which will go a long way in disciplining a Cabinet.

If we add to this a social factor, the magnitude of the Prime Minister's authority becomes enormous. This is the tremendous social prestige commanded by ministerial positions. This is a veritable weapon in the hands of the Prime Minister. He can lure his antagonists to submission with a much desired ministerial position.

There is still another power which the Prime Minister possesses. This is the power to prevent legal action against the Ministers of State during their tenure of office. Article 75 of the Constitution says: "The Ministers of State, during their tenure of office, shall not be subject to legal action without the consent of the Prime Minister."

In Japan, the Prime Minister is chosen in almost the same way as the Prime Minister of England. However, the Constitution does not require the Prime Minister to be a member of the Lower House of the Diet as is the convention in Great Britain. The Constitution prescribes that the "Prime Minister shall be designated from among the members of the Diet by a resolution of the Diet."[2] It may be presumed, therefore, that the Prime Minister may come from either House of the Diet. In practice, however, all the Prime Ministers since the beginning of the new Constitution have come from the Lower House of the Diet, that is, the House of Representatives.

In Great Britain, the House of Commons does not formally designate the Prime Minister. Each party has its clearly designated leader in the Commons and the leader of the party which gets majority in the House receives the Commission from the Queen to form the government. In Japan, on the other hand, the Prime Minister has to be formally designated by the Diet. After such designation the Emperor appoints the Prime Minister. Under the Imperial Constitution, the Emperor appointed the Prime Minister on the recommendation of an informal body of Elder Statesmen.

[1] Art. 20.   [2] Art. 67.

In designating the Prime Minister, the House of Representatives and the House of Councillors vote separately and the person securing majority in both the Houses is declared to be the choice of the Diet for premiership. If the two Houses disagree the issue is referred to a joint committee of both Houses and if the committee also fails to reach an agreement the decision of the House of Representatives is taken to be the decision of the Diet. Thus, in the designation of the Prime Minister the Lower House has been given a preponderance over the Upper House and this explains, at least partially, why the Prime Minister comes from the Lower House.

CHAPTER 6

The Diet

The concerns and needs of a political system today have grown too vast, too complex and too specialized for any body of elected popular representatives to provide effective control over anything but the broadest outlines of policy. We live in the day of the administrative state, and this is as true in Japan as it is in England, Russia, and the United States.

—Robert E. Ward

THE DIET—the national Parliament of Japan—is a bicameral body, as supreme as the British Parliament with one exception: the right of the Supreme Court to disallow unconstitutional legislation. For the rest it is now given the power of the purse without restriction and is declared to be "the highest organ of state power," and "the sole law-making organ of the state."[1] Compared to the British Parliament and the Congress of the United States, the Diet is undoubtedly very young but it is the oldest and the most experienced legislative body in Asia. "It is a parliamentary body which emerged as the inevitable result of the impact of western civilization in the late nineteenth century."[2]

Under the old Constitution of the Empire of Japan, the Emperor was more than the highest organ of state power and he combined in himself the rights of sovereignty. Although every law required the consent of the Imperial Diet the Emperor could issue ordinances which had the force of law. The ordinance-making power of the Emperor specifically limited the competence of the old Diet. Diet approval was necessary for the budget. But in case of disapproval the Cabinet could simply pass the previous year's schedule of expenditures. Declaration of war, conclusion of treaties, command of the armed forces,

[1] Art. 41.   [2] Yanaga, Chitoshi, *Japanese People and Politics*, p. 169.

48

Imperial Household management were outside the competence of the Diet.

The new Constitution of Japan, however, clearly says that sovereign power resides with the people and makes the Diet which shall consist of elected members, representative of all the people. It is the highest organ of state power and the sole law-making authority. "The government has thus been transformed from an Emperor-centred to Parliament-centred mechanism, and the elected representatives of the people have become vastly more powerful."[1]

Article 42 of the Constitution says: "The Diet shall consist of two Houses, namely the House of Representatives and the House of Councillors." The House of Representatives is the Lower House and the House of Councillors, the Upper. By the terms of Article 43 of the Constitution, the number of members of each House is to be fixed by law.

The House of Representatives

The House of Representatives now consists of 486 members returned from 123 electoral districts. Although elected for four years, the term of office of the representatives may be terminated before the full term is up in case the House of Representatives is dissolved.[2] The term of office of the members of the House of Representatives is, therefore, not determinate. And since the promulgation of the new Constitution no House survived the full term of four years.

Article 54 of the Constitution says: "When the House of Representatives is dissolved there must be a general election of the members of the House of Representatives within forty (40) days from the date of dissolution, and the Diet must be convoked within thirty (30) days from the date of the election.

The Japanese House of Representatives although it resembles the American House of Representatives is expected to be more responsive to public opinion since it is subject to dissolution.

[1] Ward, Robert E., *Japan's Political System*, p. 88.   [2] Art. 45.

The House of Councillors

General MacArthur, the Supreme Commander of the Allied Powers, was in favour of a unicameral legislature. He argued that since Japan was a unitary state it was not necessary for her to have a Senate-like Upper Chamber. Japanese officials, however, insisted on an appointive second chamber or a corporate one representing the various districts or professions as a check against the excesses of the Lower Chamber. "The present House of Councillors represents a somewhat unsatisfactory compromise between these two viewpoints."[1]

Membership and Election

The House of Councillors now consists of 250 members of whom 150 come from 46 electoral districts—each district having two to eight members roughly in proportion to population. The remaining 100 members are elected by the nation at large. In the election to the House of Councillors, therefore, a voter votes twice—once for a candidate in the electoral district and once for a candidate in the national constituency.

It was expected that since the national constituency would offer opportunities for persons of truly national stature to be elected to the Upper House of the national legislature without being involved in party politics and because of higher age qualification, the Councillors "would be superior in dignity, experience and impartiality to the Representatives." In fact, this was the justification for adopting a very "unusual and complicated" system of election.

But, as McNelly has observed: "After fifteen years of operation, however, the House of Councillors is not greatly different from the House of Representatives either in terms of age or politics. The strength of the two main parties is about identical in each House."[2]

Term of the Councillors

The Councillors are elected for 6 years, half of the members retiring every three years. This is laid down in Article 46 of

[1] Ward, *op. cit.*, p. 88.
[2] McNelly, Theodore, *Contemporary Government of Japan* (1963), p. 103.

the Constitution: "The term of office of members of the House
of Councillors shall be six years and election for half the members shall take place every three years." However, the term
of office for half the members of the House of Councillors serving in the first term shall be three years. Members falling
under this category shall be determined in accordance with
law.[1]

The House of Councillors is not subject to dissolution but,
"when the House of Representatives is dissolved, the House of
Councillors is closed at the same time. However, the Cabinet
may in time of national emergency convoke the House of
Councillors in emergency session."[2]

Munro and Ayearst observe: "American influence is seen in
the provision that one half of the Councillors retire each three
years. In another respect the House of Councillors does not
resemble our Senate. It is much inferior in power to the other
chamber."[3]

However, since the House of Councillors is not subject to
dissolution, it is expected to lend continuity and stability to
the political system.

Qualifications of the Members of the Diet

Article 44 of the Constitution says: "The qualifications of
members of both Houses and their electors shall be fixed by
law. However, there shall be no discrimination because of race,
creed, sex, social status, family origin, education, property or
income." The Constitution thus provides for universal adult
franchise.

The significance of this provision can be fully appreciated if
we keep in mind the electoral laws under the old Constitution.
Women did not have the right to vote and male voter of at
least 25 years of age had to satisfy tax qualifications. He must
have paid a minimum of 3 yen direct tax to the national ex-
chequer for more than one year and paid an income tax for
more than 3 years and have been a resident within a prefecture
for at least 6 months.

[1] Art. 102. [2] Art. 54.
[3] Munro, W. B. and Morley, A., *The Government of Europe*, p. 777.

This was the position even in 1919. However, the Universal Suffrage Act, 1925, conferred the right to vote on all males of over 25 years of age.

It was under the direction of General MacArthur that the Japanese government in 1945 provided for women suffrage and reduced the voting age from 25 to 20.

Members of the Diet have to satisfy two essential requirements, one of age and the other of geography. The age qualification is 25 years for the Representatives and 30 years for the Councillors. Geographic requirement relates to the legal residence of the Diet members in a prefecture.

Disputes related to qualifications of the Diet members are judged by the Houses themselves. "However, in order to deny a seat to any member, it is necessary to pass a resolution by a majority of two-thirds or more of the members present."[1]

The Constitution does not permit anyone to be a member of both Houses simultaneously.[2]

The Speaker and the Vice-Speaker

Each House of the Diet elects a Speaker who presides over the deliberations of the House and maintains order. A Vice-Speaker is also elected. The Speaker normally comes from the majority party in the House like his counterpart in the British House of Commons and the American House of Representatives. The Vice-Speaker, however, is frequently chosen from the ranks of the opposition. In 1958, however, the Liberal Democratic Party which held majority in the House put up its candidates for both the positions and in spite of the objections of the Socialists, got them elected.

Political neutrality of the Speaker is accepted as an ideal. But it is difficult to see how this neutrality can be maintained when the Speaker is not required by law or by convention to resign from his party as is the case in Great Britain.

However, during the 15 years from 1925 to 1940 a very healthy practice had developed. Both the Speaker and the Vice-Speaker severed their party connections. This was consequential to a resolution of the House of Representatives. But

---

[1] Art. 55.   [2] Art. 48.

this practice did not continue after 1940 although both the Speaker and the Vice-Speaker of the Sixteenth Special Diet Session resigned from their respective parties.

Since the Speaker remains a party man and behaves in a partisan way like the Speaker in the American House of Representatives, he does not command the prestige and dignity of the Speaker of the British House of Commons. He has all the powers which are incidental to the presiding officer of a House who is entrusted with the responsibility of maintaining order and discipline. But his authority is not as much as that of the British Speaker.

He is the official representative of the House. He determines the order of business, refers Bills to appropriate committees, casts his vote in case of a tie; controls debates and discussions in the House. He can admonish and censure the members for disorderly conduct and refer cases of disorderliness on the part of the members to the Disciplinary Committee of the House. And when the House becomes unruly and gets out of control he may declare a recess or adjourn the House.

He may expel disorderly spectators from the gallery of the House. If necessary the Speaker may call in police inside the House. For instance, in June, 1954, the Speaker had to call in police for the first time to put the disorderly House in order. The same had to be done again in 1960 and 1961 when the Socialists prevented the Speaker from convening the House.

Immunities of the Diet members

Like the members of the Legislature of any democratic country the Diet members in Japan are entitled to certain immunities which are universally recognized as essential for the proper discharge of legislative responsibilities. These are laid down in Articles 50 and 51 of the Constitution.

Members of the Diet are exempted from apprehension while the Diet is in session, and any member apprehended before the opening of the session must be freed during the term of the session upon demand of the House. Members of the Diet are also not held liable outside the House for speeches, debates or votes cast inside the House.

Session of the Diet

Following the convention in Great Britain, the Diet meets at least once a year. This has been constitutionally prescribed: "An ordinary session of the Diet shall be convoked once per year."[1] However, an extraordinary session may be convoked by the Cabinet and when one-fourth or more of the total members of either House makes the demand, the Cabinet must determine on such convocation.[2]

A comparable example of the legislature itself taking the initiative for an extraordinary session may be found in Switzerland where the Federal Council may convene an extraordinary session of the Federal Assembly on the request of one-fourth of the National Council or on that of 5 Cantons.

Committees of the Diet

The two Houses of the Diet function principally through their committees. There are 16 Standing Committees of each House relating to 16 principal divisions of administration. These committees are: (1) Cabinet, (2) local administration, (3) judicial affairs, (4) foreign affairs, (5) finance, (6) education, (7) welfare and labour, (8) agriculture, forestry and fisheries, (9) commerce and industry, (10) transport, (11) communications, (12) construction, (13) budget, (14) accounts, (15) steering, and (16) discipline.

Membership of these committees and their chairmanships are allocated to the parties on the basis of their relative strength in the House although since 1958, chairmanships have become a monopoly of the party in power. In the United States a committee chairman is appointed on the basis of seniority. But this principle is not followed in Japan. The chairman of a committee is normally selected by his party's high command, elected by the committee members and formally appointed by the Speaker.

In the committee meetings members of the government party see to it that a government Bill is carried through the committee while the members of the opposition resort to filibustering and other delaying tactics.

[1] Art. 52.   [2] Art. 53.

Special committees may be constituted on a temporary basis to deal with special problems. Special committees sometimes attract widespread attention and interest. This is because of the nature of the problems dealt with by them. We may refer here the special committee on the Japan-United States Security Treaty.

There is also one standing committee of both Houses of the Diet—the Legislative Committee—which consists of 18 members—10 from the Lower House and 8 from the Upper. Chairmanship rotates between the Houses. This is a general committee which deals with the problems related to Diet's powers and procedure and makes recommendations.

The Constitution also provides for a joint committee of two Houses. Such a committee consisting of 10 members from each House is mandatory under three conditions: (a) when the two disagree on the designation of the Prime Minister; (b) when the House of Councillors makes a decision different from that of the House of Representatives over the adoption of the national budget; (c) when the Houses differ on the Diet approval required for the conclusion of treaties.

According to McNelly, "The principal functions of the committee system in Japan are (1) to educate the public, since committee meetings are usually open and well publicized by the Press, and (2) to provide an arena for criticism and obstruction by the opposition."[1]

When a Bill is introduced in the House, the Speaker refers it to an appropriate committee of the House. The committee then sets on examining the Bill after which it makes a report to the House. The House then deliberates and votes on the Bill. Of course, an urgent Bill may not be referred to a committee if the Steering Committee of the House so decides.

In Great Britain, a Bill is referred to a committee only when it has been accepted by Parliament on principle and the committee must make a report on the same. In the United States, a Bill is referred to a committee before it is considered by the Congress and the committee may not report back a Bill and may pigeonhole the same. In Japan also a Bill need not be reported out if the committee deems it unnecessary, unworthy

[1] McNelly, *op. cit.*, p. 105.

or undesirable and if it fails to get majority support. However, a committee must report on a Bill if it was transmitted from the other House or when a report is demanded by 20 members.

One-third or more of the members constitute the quorum in the Diet and the decision is taken by a majority of those present, and in case of a tie, the Speaker decides the issue by exercising the casting vote.

In respect of their importance in the field of legislative business the committees of the Diet compare favourably with those of the American Congress. They are not "lame institutions" like the Standing Committees of the British House of Commons. Rather, they form "the core of legislative process in the Diet." Upon them "devolves the primary responsibility of selecting those legislative proposals submitted by the government and recommending them for approval and enactment by the Diet."[1]

Functions of the Diet

In theory, the principal function of any legislative body is the making of laws. In practice, however, the legislature does not make many laws. A vast majority of the Bills are drafted by government officials and sponsored by the Cabinet and since the Cabinet belongs to the majority party in the legislature the fate of a Bill is almost always predetermined. Therefore, it may be said that even in the exercise of its most important function the legislature is under the executive leadership.

This is true of the Diet in Japan as much as it is of the legislative bodies in most western democracies. The Constitution has made the Diet the sole law-making organ of the state. But, in fact, it does not initiate Bills. It only deliberates, debates and votes on the Bills introduced in the House by the executive. Even in debates, discussions and voting the members are not free. Since party discipline is very strictly maintained both in the committees and in the House, the members of the government party and of the opposition behave like a well-disciplined army.

In fact, the Diet members are under the pressure of business as much as their counterparts in Britain and the United States.

[1] Yanaga, *op. cit.*, pp. 195-96.

They have neither the time nor the technical knowledge to devote the needed attention to the complexities of modern legislation. Moreover, a Diet member "is also under pressure of ever-increasing and exacting demands of his constitutents".

Other important functions of the Diet include the following:

(a) Designation of the Prime Minister—who, in fact, comes from the House of Representatives—by a resolution.

(b) Control of the executive. This is effected through the power of the House of Representatives to pass a no-confidence resolution or reject a confidence resolution.

(c) Adoption of the national budget. This is considered to be the most important of all the regular activities of the Diet. The Diet decides finally both government revenues and expenditures. Without the authorization of the Diet, no taxes can be levied and no expenditures made.

By the terms of the Consitution the Cabinet prepares a budget for each fiscal year and submits it to the Diet for its consideration and decision. In order to provide for unforeseen deficiencies in the budget the Diet may authorize a reserve fund to be expended upon the responsibility of the Cabinet. The Cabinet must get subsequent approval of the Diet for all payments from the reserve fund.

There is a Board of Audit which audits annually final accounts of expenditures and revenues of the state. The Cabinet submits the same to the Diet together with the statement of the Board of Audit. Furthermore, the Cabinet bears constitutional responsibility to report at regular intervals and at least annually on the state of national finances to the Diet and the people.

The Diet controls the property of the Imperial Household. Article 8 of the Constitution says: "No property can be given to, or received by, the Imperial House, nor can any gifts be made therefrom, without the authorization of the Diet."

The Diet appropriates all expenses of the Imperial Household in the budget. Article 88 clearly lays down: "All property of the Imperial Household shall belong to the state. All expenses of the Imperial Household shall be appropriated by the Diet in the budget."

(d) Control over the conduct of foreign relations. The Prime Minister reports on foreign relations to the Diet. The Cabinet is given the power to manage foreign affairs and conclude treaties. However, the Constitution obliges the Cabinet to obtain prior or, depending on circumstances, subsequent approval of the Diet."[1] Thus, without the approval of the Diet no treaty can be effective.

In the United States also treaties become effective when ratified by the Senate. If the President is in difficulty with the Senate he may avoid a formal treaty and enter into executive agreements which do not require ratification by the Senate. In Japan also the Cabinet may conclude executive agreements independently under its general power to manage foreign affairs.

Again, as in the United States, negotiations for the conclusion of treaties may be carried on by the Cabinet and the Diet does not come in the picture at this stage. Treaties come before the Diet in their final form, that is, after the completion of negotiations. Of course, Diet approval may be sought in advance. In that case, the Diet may approve on the condition that the Cabinet settles the issues that may arise in course of negotiation.

Incidentally, it may be mentioned here that Japan took over the formal responsibility of her foreign policy since the end of the Occupation in April, 1952.

(e) Finally, the Diet is given the power to "conduct investigations in relation to government, and may demand the presence and testimony of witnesses and the production of records."[2] By the exercise of this power, the Diet may supervise the operation of the government as the legislative bodies do in both Great Britain and the United States. The supervisory and investigative function of the Diet is a new principle introduced by the new Constitution. Under the Meiji Constitution the Imperial Diet had no such power.

(f) In addition to this investigative function the Diet performs certain judicial functions also. It sets up an "impeachment court from among the members of both Houses for the purpose of trying those judges against whom removal proceedings have been instituted."[3]

[1] Art. 73.   [2] Art. 62.   [3] Art. 64.

The Diet can also act as a Constituent Assembly since amendments to the Constitution "shall be initiated by the Diet, through a concurring vote of two-thirds or more of all the members of each House and shall thereupon be submitted to the people for ratification, which shall require the affirmative vote of a majority of all votes cast thereon at a special referendum or at such election as the Diet shall specify."[1]

Relation Between the Two Houses of the Diet

The circumference of the functions of the two Houses of the Diet is the same. But the Constitution prescribes a subordinate position for the House of Councillors. It is much inferior in power to the House of Representatives.

An ordinary Bill may be introduced in either House of the Diet and it requires passage by both Houses to become a law. But in case of any disagreement between the two Houses, the opinion of the House of Representatives prevails. Article 59 of the Constitution says: "A Bill which is passed by the House of Representatives, and upon which the House of Councillors makes a decision different from that of the House of Representatives, becomes a law when passed a second time by the House of Representatives by a majority of two-thirds or more of the members present."

The House of Representatives may thus override the veto of the Upper House by a two-thirds majority. But, as Quigley and Turner observe: "It is of small consequence in view of the difficulty of obtaining a two-thirds vote, and is unlikely to be used except with relation to Bills which have received large majorities in the House of Representatives."[2]

Again, if the House of Councillors fails to take final action within sixty (60) days (time in recess excepted) after receipt of a Bill, the House of Representatives may interpret this failure as a rejection of the said Bill by the House of Councillors.[3] It must be very clear, therefore, that the power of the House of Councillors to hold up ordinary legislation is extremely limited. It cannot permanently block the passage of a Bill. It can at best delay a Bill for 60 days.

[1] Art. 96.   [2] Quigley, H. S., and Turnei, J. E., *The New Japan*, p. 240.
[3] Art. 59.

However, the Constitution provides for the meeting of a joint committee of both Houses which may be called for by the House of Representatives for solving any disagreement.[1]

The power of the House of Councillors in budgetary matters is still more restricted. The Constitution says: "The budget must first be submitted to the House of Representatives."[2] This is analogous to the provision of the American Constitution which restricts the introduction of the budget in the House of Representatives and of the British Parliament Act, 1911, which prohibits the introduction of Money Bills in the House of Lords.

The budget, after its passage through the House of Representatives, comes before the House of Councillors. The House of Councillors cannot reject or modify the budget. The Constitution says that the decision of the House of Representatives on the budget shall be the decision of the Diet (a) when the House of Councillors makes a decision different from that of the House of Representatives; (b) when no agreement can be reached even through a joint committee of both Houses; (c) when the House of Councillors fails to take action within thirty (30) days (the period of recess excluded) after the receipt of the budget.[3]

It is, therefore, seen that the power of the House of Councillors in respect of the budget is limited to its delaying the same by a maximum period of thirty (30) days.

The same applies to the Diet approval required for the conclusion of treaties.[4]

The provisions of Articles 60 and 61 were applied in 1960 at the time of the approval of the Japan-United States Security Treaty. The House of Councillors decided not to deliberate without the Socialists who were then boycotting the House. Thirty days after the approval of the Treaty by the House of Representatives the decision of the Lower House was taken to be the decision of the Diet.

It must be noted that the Senate in the United States has the exclusive power of ratification of treaties. The House of Representatives can only have an indirect influence through its control of the purse.

[1] Art. 59.   [2] Art. 60.   [3] Art. 60.   [4] Art. 61.

However, as Dr. Yanaga observes, the House of Councillors "carries greater prestige for its members." "This is", he says, "largely the result of the carry over into the new system of the prestige which was attached to the old House of Peers. Because of the very nature of the functions assigned to it and the security of tenure, the proceedings in the House of Councillors are less hectic and stormy. Members are not only more dignified but much less ambitious politically than in the Lower House. They are as a rule little older and more experienced in life, if not in politics. On the whole, they are better known nationally and a large proportion of them have been specialists."[1]

In conclusion it may be observed that the Diet constituted as it is and extensive powers given over the control and management of national affairs may be a very powerful arm of democratic government. However, this will depend upon the vitality of the political parties.

[1] Yanaga, *op. cit.*, p. 178.

CHAPTER 7

The Judiciary

There has been such a complete revamping of the Judiciary that the Courts are actually cast in an entirely new role. Under the new system the Judiciary has achieved independence in the true sense of the word. It is no longer the strong arm of the executive branch that it was under the old Constitution; it is completely independent of the executive control, intervention or pressure.

—Chistoshi Yanaga

UNDER THE old Constitution of Japan, the Judiciary was not an independent branch of the government. It was a "strong arm" of the executive. The Courts were administrative organs and exercised judicial powers as sovereign functions of the Emperor. Article 57 of the Meiji Constitution says: "The Judicature shall be exercised by the Courts of Law according to law, in the name of the Emperor." The Courts were under the supervision of the Minister of Justice. Judges were appointed and dismissed by the government. The spirit of independence of the judiciary was totally absent.

The new Constitution, however, envisages an American styled independent judiciary.

Chapter VI of the Constitution deals with the Judiciary. Article 76 says: "The whole judicial power is vested in a Supreme Court and in such inferior Courts as are established by law." The Supreme Court stands at the apex of the judicial structure and is situated in Tokyo. Below the Supreme Court there are 8 High Courts with 6 High Court branches, 49 District Courts with 235 District Court branches, all in main cities, 570 Summary Courts in 570 principal cities, towns and villages, 49 Family Courts with 235 Family Court branches, all in main cities.

The Supreme Court

Composition: Article 79 of the Constitution says: "The Supreme Court shall consist of a Chief Judge and such number of judges as may be determined by law . . . ." At present there are 15 judges in the Supreme Court bench including the Chief Judge.

Qualifications of the judges: Although the Constitution does not prescribe any qualification for the Supreme Court judges, they must be "persons of broad vision and extensive knowledge of law". They must not be less than 40 years of age. Ten (10) of the judges must have high judicial qualifications not less than twenty years' professional experience as judges, procurators or lawyers and the rest must be learned persons of experience but not necessarily in the field of law. According to Chitoshi Yanaga, "This is designed to permit a more democratic and varied representation of expertise on the highest tribunal of the nation."[1]

The old Constitution of the Empire of Japan, however, stipulated: "The judges shall be appointed from among those who possess proper qualifications according to law."[2]

Method of appointment: The method of appointment of the judges of the Supreme Court is laid down in the Constitution. Article 6 of the Constitution says: "The Emperor shall appoint the Chief Judge of the Supreme Court as designated by the Cabinet." This procedure is designed to accord to the Chief Judge a status comparable to that of the Prime Minister who is also appointed by the Emperor on being designated by the Diet. The fourteen other judges are appointed by the Cabinet.[3] Their appointment is attested by the Emperor.

Incidentally it may be mentioned here that in pre-war Japan the Chief Justice of the old Supreme Court ranked below the Minister of Justice. Today the Chief Justice ranks with the Prime Minister and the presiding officers of the Houses of the Diet. The new Constitution thus elevates the status of the Chief Justice of the Supreme Court.

The judges of the English Courts are appointed by the Queen and since the Queen is a constitutional head and acts on the

[1] Yanaga, Chitoshi, *Japanese People and Politics*, p. 356.
[2] Art. 58.   [3] Art. 79

advice of her Ministers, Cabinet influence in judicial appointments is obvious. In the United States, the judges of the Supreme Court are appointed by the President with the consent of the Senate. The judges of the Swiss Federal Tribunal are elected for a 6-year term by the two chambers of the Federal Assembly in a joint session. The judges of the Supreme Court of the U.S.S.R. are also elected by the Supreme Soviet of the U.S.S.R. for a term of five years.

Inferior Courts

High Courts: High Courts are basically appellate courts. They hear appeals and complaints from judgments and rulings of the District or Family Courts. High Courts vary in membership and may sit as full benches or in groups of three or five judges.

District Courts: District Courts "constitute the principal trial courts and exercise a general jurisdiction over all civil actions not specifically given to other courts." The entire country is divided into 49 judicial districts in each of which there is a District Court. District Courts also hear appeals and complaints from the Summary Courts. Normally, a single judge sits on a District Court but serious cases are tried by a body of 3 judges.

The Supreme Court, the High Courts and the District Courts replace the former Supreme Court, Courts of Appeal and district courts.

Summary Courts: On the lowest rung of the judicial ladder stand the Summary Courts and the Family Courts. The Summary Courts "represent an innovation designed to simplify judicial procedure at the lowest level and to overcome the public attitude of awe, if not distrust, toward the courts as well as to do away with the stigma attached to litigation by encouraging the use of courts."[1] The Summary Courts try minor civil and criminal cases by summary procedure. These courts are uniformly presided over by a single judge.

Family Courts: These two types of courts—the Summary Courts and the Family Courts—are entirely new. The Family

[1] Yanaga, *op. cit.*, p. 357.

Courts are designed to promote harmonious relationship within the family and among relatives. The Family Court, ·therefore, functions "as much as a social welfare institution as it does a court." Burks is of opinion that "the Family Court offers the greatest promise of becoming Japan's outstanding court of the people and for the people."[1] Family Court, he says, is "the most unusual development in the Japanese Court system."[2]

The Family Courts apply "not only law but also the community conscience and the latest findings of the social sciences." "It is only natural," observes Burks, "that modern Japanese judicial procedure would reflect the traditional emphasis on the family as a critical realm of social control and that the present organization of courts would also provide a unique institution handling family problems."[3] A single judge normally, though not always, presides over Family Courts.

In Great Britain lay men are associated with the courts as jurors. In Japan lay men come into association with the Family Courts as counsellors and conciliators.

The judges of the inferior courts are appointed by the Cabinet from a list of persons nominated by the Supreme Court. They must also satisfy high qualifications but no minimum age is prescribed either by the Constitution or by a statute. They hold office for a term of ten (10) years and are eligible for reappointment.[4] However, the judges of the High Courts and District Courts must retire at the age of 65 while those of the Summary Courts at the age of 70.

Public Procurators

At every level of the Japanese court system there is a procurator's office. The function of a public procurator is to represent the state in criminal cases. At the head of the entire system stands the procurator-general. The procurators are appointed by the Minister of Justice from among highly qualified persons. Their salaries are fixed by statute. The procurator-general retires at the age of 65 while other procurators retire at the

[1] Burks, A. W., *The Government of Japan*, p. 172. [2] *Ibid.*, p. 171.
[3] *Ibid.*, p. 159. [4] Art. 80.

age of 63. The public procurators although subject to the rule-making power of the Supreme Court are administrative officials and are under the control and supervision of the Minister of Justice.

Since Japan is a unitary state there is only one integrated system of courts and no separate system of courts for local governments.

Court Procedure

In Japan trials are conducted and judgments declared publicly unless a court decides otherwise. However, cases involving political offences and the infringement of civil rights must always be tried in public.

Article 82 of the Constitution says: "Trials shall be conducted and judgment declared publicly. Where a court unanimously determines publicity to be dangerous to public order or morals, a trial may be conducted privately, but trials of political offences involving the Press or cases wherein the rights of people as guaranteed in Chapter III of the Constitution are in question shall always be conducted publicly."

The old Constitution also provided for public trials. But whereas the new Constitution leaves it entirely to the courts to decide if such trials are dangerous to public order or morals and makes exceptions in cases involving political offences and infringement of civil rights, the old Constitution says that public trials may be suspended by provision of law or by the decision of the Court of Law without any exception. Article 59 of the old Constitution reads as follows: "Trials and judgments of a court shall be conducted publicly. When, however, there exists any fear that such publicity may be prejudicial to peace and order, or to the maintenance of public morality, the public trial may be suspended by provision of law or by the decision of the Court of Law."

No Extraordinary Tribunal

In line with the Anglo-American practice, separate administrative court system has been abolished. The ordinary courts now try cases involving alleged breaches of law by officials. Article 76 of the Constitution says: "No extraordinary tribunal shall be established, nor shall any organ or agency of the Executive be given final judicial power." This shall satisfy the second principle of Dicey's Rule of Law.

Every Japanese, irrespective of his social, economic or political position, shall be subject to the same ordinary law of the land administered by the same ordinary law courts. In France, administrative tribunals still prevail. Public officials while acting in their official capacity are immune from the jurisdiction of ordinary law courts. Their relations with private citizens are also determined by a body of special rules known as administrative rules. These special rules, again, are interpreted and administered by special tribunals known as administrative tribunals. The new Constitution of Japan does not permit the establishment of such special tribunals or any special treatment for public officials.

The old Constitution of Japan provided for a special court to deal with matters specially provided for by law and a Court of Administrative Litigation to deal with alleged illegal acts of administrative officers or agencies.

Article 60: All matters that fall within the competency of a special court shall be specially provided for by law.

Article 61: No suit at law, which relates to rights alleged to have been infringed by the illegal measures of the administrative authorities, and which shall come within the competency of the Court of Administrative Litigation specially established by law, shall be taken cognizance of by a Court of Law.

Under the influence of the American Occupation authorities Japan dispensed with its Court of Administrative Litigation.

However, the Japanese people are not very much enthusiastiy about their courts. The traditional attitude of the people is to settle their disputes out of court. They are indifferent, if not averse, to their courts. They look upon the court as a "place frequented by wrong doers," the procurator's office as "the enemy of the people," and the lawyers as "friends and defenders of evil men." ●

In the words of Robert E. Ward: "The Japanese are a rather remarkably nonlitigious people. They are traditionally suspicious of the courts and of formal legal processes, and have a pronounced preference for settling disputes by informal methods of conciliation and mediation."[1] Dr. Yanaga observes: "No serious efforts have been made as yet to bring the courts closer to the people and to win their confidence and support."[2] The result is, the traditional attitude of indifference to litigative process still prevails.

Popular Review of the Judges

But the most unique and peculiar feature of the Japanese judicial system is the device of recall for the popular determination of the fitness of the judges. Article 79 of the Constitution says:

"The appointment of the judges of the Supreme Court shall be reviewed by the people at the first general election of members of the House of Representatives following their appointment, and shall be reviewed again at the first general election of members of the House of Representatives after a lapse of ten (10) years, and in the same manner thereafter . . . when the majority of the voters favours the dismissal of a judge, he shall be dismissed."

Admittedly, this system of popular review of the judges might produce certain unfortunate consequences. The judges might be dragged into the vortex of partisan politics. Their decisions might be politically biased with an eye to their future approval of tenure. The pressure groups might use this system in their attempts to sway judicial opinions. On the other hand, it is also understandable that a judge is liable to be dismissed by the majority of the voters only when he gives an extremely unpopular judgment affecting a vast majority of them and causing widespread resentment.

This may happen only on very rare occasions. Actually, however, not a single judge has ever been dismissed by the voters and in every case of popular review of the judges the percentage of favourable voters was as high as 90 per cent. J.M. Maki, therefore, observes that the system of popular review of the

---

[1] Ward Robert E., *Japan's Political System*, p. 102.   [2] *Ibid.*, p. 363.

judges of the Supreme Court "has proved to be largely mean-
ingless" and seems "to be the most dispensable item in the
Constitution."[1]

Judges of the Supreme Court retire at the age of 70 unless
removed earlier by public impeachment or judicially declared
mentally or physically incompetent to perform official duties.

Independence of the Judiciary

The Constitution says: "All judges shall be independent in
the exercise of their conscience and shall be bound only by this
Constitution and the laws."[2] The independence of the judiciary
from executive control is ensured by the provision of the Constitution that no "disciplinary action against judges shall be
administered by any executive organ or agency."[3]

But the most important thing that determines the independence of any functionary is the remuneration that he receives.
The new Constitution guarantees that judges "shall receive, at
regular intervals, adequate compensation which shall not be
decreased during their terms of office."[4]

This guarantee seems to be absolute. The Constitution does
not refer to any special circumstance or situation when the
salary of the judges may be reduced. Incidentally, it may be
mentioned here that although the judges of the Indian courts
enjoy similar guarantees, in times of financial emergency the
President may issue directions for the reduction of salaries and
allowances of the judges of the Supreme Court and High Courts.
(Article 360/4/6).

Not only shall the Supreme Court be free from legislative
and executive control but the Court shall have complete control over all judicial affairs of the country and the administration of justice, the legislature and the executive being totally
excluded from any share. This is clear from Article 77 of the
Constitution which lays down:

"The Supreme Court is vested with the rule-making power
under which it determines the rules of procedure and of practice, and of matters relating to attorneys, the internal discipline

---

[1] Maki, J. M., *Government and Politics in Japan*, p. 106.
[2] Art. 76.   [3] Art. 78.   [4] Art. 79.

of the courts and the administration of judicial affairs. Public procurators shall be subject to the rule-making power of the Supreme Court."

The Supreme Court exercises this control through the Legal Research and Training Institute, established by law under the jurisdiction of the Supreme Court. "No one can become a lawyer, a judge, or a public procurator unless he has either been graduated from the Institute or, in a few cases, has undergone a course of in-service training there. This gives the Supreme Court control over the entry into the legal profession and thus the power to determine over the years the nature of the entire system of the administration of justice. The Supreme Court also operates similar institutes for the training of court clerks and family court probation officers."[1]

But the point is, in a democracy no branch of the government should remain beyond accountability and be left completely unchecked. The government and its branches must operate under a system of checks and balances. In Japan also, apart from the popular review of the judges, we must remember that it is the Cabinet which designates the Chief Justice of the Supreme Court for appointment by the Emperor and appoints other associate judges of the Supreme Court and the judges of the inferior courts and that the Diet has the power to set up Impeachment Court.

Judicial Review

The new Constitution of Japan has adopted an unfamiliar concept—the American doctrine of judicial review—which means examination of legislative statutes and executive or administrative acts by the judiciary to determine whether or not they are valid in terms of the Constitution. Article 81 of the Constitution makes the Supreme Court the "court of last resort" and confers upon it the power "to determine the constitutionality of any law, order, regulation or official act". The Supreme Court is thus designed to operate as the guardian of the Constitution.

[1] Maki, *op. cit.*, p. 105.

The Japanese Supreme Court is, therefore, more powerful than either the Swiss Federal Tribunal, the Supreme Court of the U.S.S.R. or the British Courts.

The Federal Tribunal in Switzerland and the Supreme Court of the U.S.S.R. are denied the power of judicial review. In Switzerland, the theory is, the people should have the power of accepting or rejecting a piece of legislation. In the Soviet Union, on the other hand, judicial review has been found to be incompatible with the dictatorial rule. The British Courts are also helpless against the legislature. The people rely so much on legislative supremacy that even an apparently absurd law, if duly passed by the Parliament, cannot be invalidated by the Courts.

The Americans, however, were apprehensive of both executive and legislative tyranny and empowered their courts accordingly. It is only natural that a. Constitution prepared under American influence should constitute the courts both against the legislature and the executive.

But, while the American Supreme Court derives its power of judicial review from its own interpretation of the Constitution, the Supreme Court in Japan has been explicitly granted this power by the Constitution. However, the Japanese Supreme Court like its American counterpart determines the constitutional validity of laws only when specific complaints are made to the Court.

Again, while the judges of the American Supreme Court decide questions of constitutionality by a simple majority vote the requirement in Japan is that such questions are to be decided with the approval of more than eight (8) judges and not by a simple majority.

The power of judicial review has been described by Quigley and Turner as a "wholly unprecedented arrow in the judicial quiver."[1] "In the words of Ward: "This is completely foreign to the Japanese legal tradition and many have watched with interest to see whether or not the Supreme Court would actually make use of this power and occasionally declare any act of the Diet, of a Ministry, or of a local government unconstitutional, thus asserting its right to play a positive role in na-

[1] Quigley, Harold S. and Turner, John E., *The New Japan*, p. 368.

tional politics in the way that the United States Supreme Court does."[1]

The Supreme Court, however, has never in fact held any law, order, regulation or official act unconstitutional. The Supreme Court is of the opinion that "to declare such acts unconstitutional would be a violation of the principle of separation of powers, as well as of the doctrine of legislative supremacy; the proper remedy for legislation not clearly unconstitutional is a political one—that is, the sovereign people can pass judgment on the Diet and on the Cabinet by means of the ballot."[2]

[1] *Ibid.,* p. 102.   [2] Maki, *op. cit.,* pp. 107-08.

CHAPTER 8

Rights and Duties of the People

The Chapter on rights and duties of the people not only provides for most items found in the classical Bill of Rights, but also elevates social and economic rights of recent origin to the rank of fundamental rights.

—Yanagi Kenzo

THE USUAL practice is to incorporate a Bill of Rights in a democratic constitution. The purpose is to withdraw the rights of the people from the "vicissitudes of political controversy, to place them beyond the reach of majorities and officials and to establish them as legal principles to be applied by the courts."[1] Since the rights are fundamental and sacred they cannot be submitted to vote and allowed to depend on the outcome of elections. Duties are not specifically mentioned because the rights are supposed to imply duties. However, the Soviet and the new Constitution of Japan make specific references to the duties of the people.

Chapter III of the new Constitution of Japan deals with the rights and duties of the people. This Chapter is much more specific and comprehensive than can be found in any of the democratic constitutions of the world. It makes an impressive list of the rights of the people in extreme earnestness. "The list goes far beyond even the American Bill of Rights, including, for example, rights of academic freedom, collective bargaining and employment."[2] This part of the Constitution has been described as "the crux of the new political system" and is "far and away the longest and the most important portion of the entire document."[3] Out of a total of 103 Articles in the

[1] U. S. Supreme Court in West Virginia State Board of Education V Barnette, 1943.   [2] Burks, *The Government of Japan*, p. 20.
[3] Yanaga, Chitoshi, *Japanese People and Politics*, p. 352.

73

Constitution no less than 31 are devoted to the rights and duties of the people.

It must be remembered that the Japanese tradition was thoroughly authoritarian. The detailed and specific enumeration of all the rights pertaining to citizenship will go a long way in building up liberal traditions in "new" Japan. In the words of Robert E. Ward, Chapter III of the Constitution represents the most "ambitious constitutional statements of the rights and duties of the people."[1] In the words of Dr. Yanaga, "Even a cursory reading of the Bill of Rights will leave no doubt in the reader's mind that this portion of the Constitution is the crux of the new political system."[2]

Article 97 of the Constitution says: "The fundamental human rights by this Constitution guaranteed to the people of Japan are the fruits of the age-old struggle of man to be free; they have survived the many exacting tests for durability and are conferred upon this and future generations in trust, to be held for all times inviolate." The rights under the new Constitution are, therefore, "eternal and inviolate."

Article 13 of the Constitution guarantees to all their right to life, liberty and the pursuit of happiness "which shall be the supreme consideration in legislation and in other governmental affairs".

Equality before the law is guaranteed by Article 14 of the Constitution which forbids discrimination in political, economic or social relations because of race, creed, sex, social status or family origin. The Constitution abolishes special privilege. It does not recognize "peers and peerage" and does not allow any privilege to follow from any award of honour, decoration or any distinction and precludes the validity of such distinction beyond the lifetime of the individual who now holds or hereafter may receive it.

The Constitution recognizes the inalienable rights of the people to choose their public officials who are the servants of the whole community and not of any group and to dismiss them. In making choice for the public officials a voter is not

[1] Ward, Robert E., *Japan's Political System*, p. 84.
[2] Yanaga, *op. cit.*, p. 351.

answerable, publicly or privately. Universal adult suffrage is guaranteed and voting is to be by secret ballot.[1]

Right to petition for the redress of grievances is thought to be an inalienable right of the citizens in a democracy. Under the new Constitution of Japan every person without any discrimination is entitled to have "the right of peaceful petition for the redress of damage, for the removal of public officials, for the enactment, repeal or amendment of laws, ordinances or regulations and for other matters."[2] In case a damage is done to a person through the illegal act of any public official, the person concerned may sue for redress from the state or public entity.[3]

Involuntary servitude is incidental to autocracy and authoritarianism. The Constitution, therefore, prohibits involuntary servitude except as punishment for crime.[4]

Secularism is involved in the very idea of a democratic and civilized state. The Constitution devotes two Articles to maintain the secular character of the state. Article 19 says that freedom of thought and conscience shall not be violated and Article 20 guarantees freedom of religion to all. Religious organizations receive no privilege from the state nor exercise any political authority. No person can be compelled to take part in any religious act, celebration, rite or practice. The state and its organs are not allowed to give any religious education or undertake any other religious activity. On December 15, 1945, by an order of the Supreme Commander for Allied Powers state religion (Shinto) was abolished altogether. Article 89 of the Constitution says: No public money or other property shall be expended or appropriated for the use, benefit or maintenance of any religious institution or association, or for any charitable, educational or benevolent enterprises not under the control of public authority.

The Constitution guarantees freedom of assembly and association as well as speech and all other forms of expression. No censorship is allowed. Nor can the secrecy of any means of communication be violated.[5] Every person is free to choose and change his residence and to choose his occupation. But

[1] Art. 15.   [2] Art. 16.   [3] Art. 17.   [4] Art. 18.   [5] Art. 21.

this freedom must not interfere with public welfare. All persons are free to move to a foreign country and to divest themselves of their nationality.[1]

The right to own or to hold property is inviolable. But this right is defined by law in conformity with public welfare. Private property may be taken for public purpose upon just compensation therefor.[2] Thus the Constitution seeks to balance the enjoyment of freedom by the individual and the good of the community as a whole.

Article 24 of the Constitution seeks to recognize the basic social and family relationships by the recognition of respect for the individual, by the acceptance of mutual consent of both sexes as the basis of marriage and its maintenance "through mutual co-operation with equal rights of husband and wife as a basis".

The Constitution directs the law-makers to enact laws with regard to the choice of spouse, property rights, inheritance, choice of domicile, divorce and other matters pertaining to marriage and the family from the standpoint of individual dignity and the essential equality of the sexes.

Quigley and Turner observe: "Article 24 may be termed the heart of the new Bill of Rights, since it sets up principles incompatible with the feudal type of family system, which was deeply imbedded in the law and customs of Japan."[3]

Three sacred rights of workers—"to organize, to bargain and act collectively"—are recognized by the Constitution although qualified by the provision that these rights may not be used in contravention of the public welfare.[4]

The Constitution guarantees the right of all people to maintain "the minimum standards of wholesome and cultured living" and obliges the state to endeavour for the promotion and extension of social welfare and security, and of public health.[5] All people are entitled to receive "an equal education correspondent to their ability". Ordinary education for all boys and girls is compulsory and free.[6]

The Constitution recognizes the right of the people to work. Standards of wages, hours, rest and other working conditions

[1] Art. 22.   [2] Art. 29.
[3] Quigley, Harold S. & Turner, John E., *The New Japan*, pp. 179-80.
[4] Art. 28.   [5] Art. 25.   [6] Art. 26.

are to be fixed by law. Exploitation of children is strictly prohibited by the Constitution.[1]

The new Constitution seeks to eliminate the abuses of the old legal and judicial system. No less than 10 Articles are devoted to this purpose. American "due process of law" has been drawn upon to support substantive with procedural right. Articles 31-39 guarantee that no person shall be deprived of life or liberty, nor shall any other criminal penalty be imposed, except according to procedure established by law; no person shall be denied the right of access to the courts; no person shall be arrested or detained without being at once informed of the charges against him or without the immediate privilege of counsel; nor shall he be detained without cause which, upon demand of any person, must be immediately shown in open court in his presence and the presence of his counsel.

The right of all persons to be secure in their homes, papers and effects against entries, searches and seizures shall not be impaired except upon warrant issued by a competent judicial officer. The infliction of torture and cruel punishment are absolutely forbidden.

In criminal cases an accused person enjoys the right to a speedy and public trial by an impartial judicial tribunal. He enjoys full opportunity to examine all witnesses, to obtain witnesses on his behalf and the assistance of competent counsel at public expense. No person can be compelled to testify against himself or convicted on confession made under compulsion, torture or threat, or after prolonged arrest or detention or solely on his own confession of guilt. No person is criminally liable for an act which was lawful at the time it was committed, or of which he has been acquitted. Nor can he be placed in double jeopardy.

These Articles are supported by Articles 17 and 40 of the Constitution. Under Article 17 a person may sue for redress from the state or public entity in case he has suffered damage through illegal act of any public official and under Article 40 he can sue the state for redress as provided by law in case he is acquitted after he has been arrested or detained.

[1] Art. 27.

These rights and freedoms are balanced by a small but significant list of duties. The people must maintain their rights and freedoms by constant endeavour, refrain from any abuse of these freedoms and rights and are responsible for utilizing them for public welfare.[1] Along with their right to work the people also carry the obligation to work. The people are also liable to taxation as provided by law.

It will be understood that far greater emphasis has been placed on the rights of the people than on their duties. The purpose is to encourage democratic development and to "effectively counteract the altogether too powerful influence of the authoritarian tradition and its legacies in Japanese society".[2]

---

[1] Art. 12.   [2] Yanaga, *op. cit.*, p. 353.

CHAPTER 9

Political Parties

The parliamentary cabinet system of government, in which the executive branch is formally responsible to the legislative branch and indirectly to the people—the form of government which prevails in Great Britain and many other democratic countries—is operating effectively in Japan.

—Theodore McNelly

POLITICAL PARTIES are indispensable to a system of parliamentary government. They help in the articulation of public opinion on specific and general issues and try to make parliamentary democracy really a government by public opinion. They present their programmes to the people and try to influence a majority of them to form the government. It is through the government that the political parties seek to translate their policies into action. "Without parties to define alternative policies and sponsor candidates for office, it would be virtually impossible for the population in a large nation to express a mandate for a given programme or for a given candidate. Parties serve as the link between the voters and the government."[1]

But a political party is not a clique or a faction which serves only private interests: it is a public political organization which serves public or general interest. However, political parties in Japan still display their pre-war characteristics. They remain organizations of politicians, officialdoms and big business as before rather than mass organizations. They are still plagued by "internal personal and ideological factionalism" which explain in a large measure the switch over of politicians from one party to another. The people, therefore, look upon the politicians as corrupt, self-seeking and uninterested in the public welfare. Munro and Ayearst observe:

[1] McNelly, Theodore, *Contemporary Government of Japan*, p. 148.

"When the Japanese parties began to reorganize under the new Constitution they again displayed the characteristics of the pre-war parties: a group of parliamentarians with supporters and associates among business men, landlords and the bureaucracy, all co-operating to further their own special interests and enjoy the fruits of power with little genuine support among the general electorate."[1]

This applies particularly to the ruling Liberal Democratic Party. The party has close connections with big business interests which exercise a very substantial measure of control over its policies. The Liberal Democratic Party is viewed as "a loose coalition of factions united for purposes of campaign and legislative strategy, rather than as a unified national party." These factions are based on "considerations of personal loyalty and advantage rather than principle or policy."[2]

In pre-war Japan lack of confidence of the people in the political parties and politicians paved the way for militarism and fascism. Today it constitutes a formidable challenge to the future of democracy.

Political parties in Japan first appeared in 1881. Earlier attempts to organize political parties were unsuccessful. As for example, in January, 1874, a nationalistic political association called the Patriotic Public Party was organized by Itagaki. But the government did not recognize it and was successful in suppressing it only after two months, that is, in March, 1874.

Japan's first political party, the Liberal Party, was founded under the presidentship of Itagaki in October, 1881. It was the vanguard of a movement for popular representative government. In the following year Japan witnessed the establishment of two more political parties, the Reform Party of Okuma which advocated the ideas of British liberalism and the Imperial Party of Ito, an extremely conservative party. While these three parties were engaged in the struggle for power the government was determined to crush them by a ruthless policy of suppression and in less than three years' time the parties were found in complete disintegration.

[1] McNelly, Theodore, *The Governments of Europe*, p. 780.
[2] Ward, Robert E., *Japan's Political System*, p. 65.

The first party government in Japan appeared in 1898. With the assassination of Premier Inukai party government came to an end in May, 1932, and in 1940, political parties were abolished. However, political parties emerged after the end of World War II. "The directive of October 4, 1945, issued by the Supreme Commander for the Allied Powers abrogating and suspending all laws, orders, and regulations restricting the freedom of thought, religion, assembly, association, speech, and Press was the green light for the resumption of political activities which had been stifled if not actually forbidden during the war."[1]

In Japan, as in the United States, political parties were looked upon with disfavour and distrust. In the United States in spite of the warnings issued by the founding fathers of the Constitution against the divisive role of the political parties, political parties did grow up and come to be an essential and the most important part of the political system. In Japan also, with the introduction of parliamentary democracy by the Constitution of 1947 political parties became an effective instrument of popular government.

However, political parties in Japan are as extra-constitutional as they are in the United States and Great Britain. There is no mention of political parties in the Constitution itself although the assumption is quite obvious. The Constitution establishes a responsible parliamentary government which necessarily involves the existence and operation of political parties. But Japan has failed to develop a two-party system which is considered essential for the smooth and efficient running of parliamentary government and for achieving political stability. The existence of multi-party system in Japan, observes Dr. Yanaga, is the product of national character and conditions," and, therefore, he is of opinion: "Before a truly two-party system could emerge and endure in Japan, it would be necessary to bring about other more basic changes in ideas and attitudes not only with regard to and in the parties but in the social milieu."[2]

The principal political parties in Japan today are the following: the Liberal Democratic Party (a conservative pro-Western

[1] Yanaga, Chitoshi, *Japanese People and Politics*, p. 234.   [2] *Ibid.*, p. 238.

party), the Socialist Party, the Komeito (or, the Clean Government Party), the (moderate) Democratic Socialist Party and the Communist Party.

The Liberal Democratic Party was formed in November, 1955. It was the result of a merger of the two conservative parties—the Liberal Party and the Democratic Party. "Despite its glittering name, the Liberal Party was far to the Right among conservative groups . . . . The Democrats were, however, only a little less conservative and differed on minor points from the Liberal Party."[1] Kishi Nobusuke, who was the principal organizer of the Liberal Democratic Party, became the Secretary-General and in February, 1957, was designated Prime Minister.

The Japan Socialist Party was formally organized in November, 1945, and from the very beginning it represented the forces on the Left. "Almost every shade of Utopian, Fabian and Marxian Socialism was represented in the membership."[2] For a very brief period from May 1947 to February 1948, the party formed the first Socialist government in Japan's history under the premiership of Katayama Tetsu. Unfortunately for the Socialists, Japan's economy was at a low ebb at that time. The government was unable to meet the economic problems and when the Left-wing Socialists opposed the financial policies of the government it fell in 1948.

The Socialist Party seems to have appeal to wage earners, intellectuals and the lower middle class in the urban areas. It also claims to speak for the small land-owners, tenants and agricultural workers.

The Komeito was formed in 1963 as the political arm of the Buddhist religious organization Sokagakkai. It raised the slogan that it was out to clean up all political corruption. Daisaku Ikeda, President of Sokagakkai, has said: "The aim of our Sokagakkai election activities is the realization of the great ideal of Nichiren, the fusion of politics and religion."[3]

The emergence of the Komei Party thus disproves the statement of Dr. Chitoshi Yanaga that in Japan parties cannot

---

[1] Burks, Ardath W.,*The Government of Japan*, p. 75.
[2] McNelly, *op. cit.*, p. 123.   [3] Quoted by Sivapali Wickremansinghe.

and do not use religion for political purposes, that there are no religious blocks and no religiously dominated parties.[1]

Sivapali Wickremansinghe traces the origin of the Komei Party to a political and economic vacuum created by Japan's defeat in World War II. He says: "Following Japan's defeat, the country was in the grip of poverty and the people had to start all over again. And the standard of public service was extremely low.

It is in these circumstances of a political and economic vacuum that many Japanese jumped at religion in expectation of tangible rewards. The Japanese by tradition are inclined to seek favours from religion in this world. What Sokagakkai preached was something to this effect: "By joining Sokagakkai and conscientiously keeping the faith, you will be reborn a happy and prosperous man."

Many Japanese believed and joined.[2]

The Democratic Socialist Party was formally founded on January 24, 1960, by the dissidents of the former Social Democratic Party of Japan which was organized in October, 1955, by reuniting the Left and Right-wing Socialists. From 1955 to 1959 the party was tormented by factional rivalry. Finally, in October, 1959, the Nishio Suehiro faction left the party in protest against the domination of the Left-wing Socialists with the declared intention to found a "genuine" Socialist Party.

Nishio Suehiro is reported to have told his supporters at the first meeting of the party in January, 1960:

"The Socialist Party suffers from the illusion that a Marxist revolution is possible in Japan. The conservative Liberal Democratic Party degenerates into political agents of big business.

"The goal of our party is to give political expressions to the aspirations of a vast segment of the nation including impoverished farmers, fishermen, and small business men whose voices have not been heeded by either the Liberal Democrats or the Socialists.

"We recognize that the society in which we live today is a capitalistic one . . . .

[1] Yanaga, *op. cit.*, p. 237.
[2] "Japan's Fringe Party Komeito," *Amrita Bazar Patrika*, June 3, 1969.

"Our party intends to achieve socialism through democratic methods, and the essence of democracy is the belief in the value of dissension and of efforts of persuasion."[1]

In conformity with this principle of achieving socialism through democratic means the Democratic Socialist Party, although opposed to the Japan-U.S. Security Treaty, did not resort to violence as did the Socialists to oppose the renewal of the Treaty in 1960.

The Japan Communist Party was reorganized in October, 1945, by some veteran Communist leaders who were released from imprisonment on the order of the Supreme Commander for the Allied Powers. But the party made itself widely unpopular by openly demanding the trial of the Emperor as a war criminal and the abolition of the institution. The Communists were the only group in the Diet to vote against the draft new Constitution.

The influence of the party was at its peak in 1949 when it won 10 per cent of the votes and 35 seats in the House of Representatives. The success of the Communist Party may be attributed to the widespread discontent with the Katayama and Ashida Ministries. The party derives its "principal support from the urban electorate, with some appeal to the tenantry and small proprietors in the rural areas". The Korean minority in Japan is another source of Communist strength "who have never forgotten nor forgiven their exploitation by the Japanese and racial discrimination they have endured".

The fortune of the Communist Party, however, declined after 1949. In 1953 only one Communist member was elected to the Lower House of the national legislature. In 1955, the Communist Party won 2 seats, in 1958 one, and in 1960 (20th November) only 3 and the same number in the General Election of 1963 (21st November).

Munro and Ayearst observe: "Immediately after the war the Communists tried to form a mass party on the French or Italian model. They advocated mild reforms (many of them identical with those advocated by SCAP) and stressed genuine

[1] *The Japan Times*, January 25, 1960. Quoted by McNelly, p. 131.

grievances. But they were handicapped by universal anti-Russian sentiment and their reputation for atheism."[1]

The Liberal Democratic Party is in charge of the administration of the government virtually since the end of the war. The General Election of 1969 also has given the Liberal Democratic Party an absolute majority. Out of 486 seats in the House of Representatives it has captured as many as 302.

The Liberal Democratic Party has gained not only in terms of seats but also in terms of popular votes. The spectacular victory of the Liberal Democratic Party has been, however, at the cost of the chief Opposition party—Japan Socialist Party—whose strength is now reduced from 134 to 90. The largest party in the House of Representatives is the religious Buddhist Party, the Komeito, with a strength of 47 seats, the same number it held before this election. The Democratic Socialist Party comes next with a strength of 31 seats. The Communist Party though not a significant force in Japanese politics has, however, been able to improve its position. From a mere 4 seats in the House of Representatives it has increased its strength to 14.

The factors that contributed to the success of the Liberal Democratic Party of Premier Eisaku Sato are the conclusion of the Japan-U.S. Security Treaty and the reversion of Okinawa (By an agreement reached between Premier Sato and President Nixon on November 21, 1969, the United States would return Okinawa to Japan in 1972, remove nuclear weapons from the strategic Pacific island but would retain military bases on Okinawa to support conventional military operation in Asia and the Far East) and the country's favourable economic position. Prime Minister Sato may take the results of the election as an expression of confidence of the people in his government.

In the last General Election the ruling conservative party had won 277 seats. The results of the 1969 election, therefore, represent a solid gain of 25 seats for the party. These together with 47 Buddhist Komeito and 31 Right-wing Democratic Socialists make a formidable total of 380. As against these forces on the Right, the forces on the Left are composed of 90 Socialists and 14 Communists.

[1] Munro and Morley, *op. cit.*, p. 781.

The developing countries in Asia may welcome the results of the 1969 election because of Mr. Sato's interest in their economic development. In the fiscal year 1969 his government contributed $ 20 million to the Asian Development Bank. The newspaper Yomiuri reports on February 15, 1970, that the Japanese government will contribute $ 36 million in the fiscal year 1970. The government has set a target of 4 billion annual aid by 1975 and 6 billion by 1980.

With increased popular support, it is expected that Mr. Sato will fulfil his pledge to play a greater role in the economic development of Asia more confidently. Premier Sato believes that only by cultivating closer ties with the Asian countries can Japan hope to check the growing influence of Communist China in Asia. He wants to accelerate his country's weight and prestige in international politics which applies specially to Asia.

Premier Eisaku Sato stands for "partnership with the United States to safeguard the stability of Asia and the economic growth of the developing nations". His party is also in favour of "retention of the Security Treaty under which the United States maintains bases in Japan as a deterrent to war in the Far East".[1] The ruling Liberal Democratic Party considers the Security Treaty to be a pillar in Japan's external relations.

The domestic and the foreign policy of the Liberal Democratic Party as formulated in the late 1950's is as follows:

"To adhere to parliamentarianism, eliminate undemocratic activities, stabilize farm and fisheries management on the principles of free enterprise; to secure the structural improvement of medium and smaller enterprises, improvement of roads, flood prevention, stabilization of national economy, effective enforcement of the social security system."

"To contribute to world peace and to elevate Japan's international status through co-operation with the free nations; to adhere to the policies of the United Nations, and maintain good-neighbourly relations with the Asian countries."[2]

The Socialist Party is opposed to the pro-Western foreign policy of Japan. It advocates "unarmed neutrality instead of

---

[1] Tokashi oka: "Japan's Revived Self-Confidence", *Amrita Bazar Patrika*, January 14, 1970,

[2] *The Japan Times*, May 7, 1959. Quoted by Burks, p. 79.

American bases in Japan". The Communist Party advocates the abrogation of the Japan-United States Security Treaty and demands withdrawal of American forces from Japan. The Democratic Socialist Party rejects the policy of neutralism, advocates the gradual modification of the Security Treaty and eventual withdrawal of American forces. Democratic Socialists also favour co-operation with the free world through the United Nations.

The results of the 1969 election, however, prove that the majority of the voters are not very much in favour of changing the nature of their security arrangements.

Vice-Foreign Minister Nobuhiko Ushiba wrote in the August 1969 edition of the monthly review Sekai no Ugoki (World Currents): "Needless to say the Japanese government intends to continue the Treaty after 1970. Moreover, according to a recent public opinion poll conducted by the Prime Minister's office, the majority of the Japanese people have expressed approval of retaining the Treaty . . . . Heated discussions on the subject will no doubt continue and some disturbances might occur. Nevertheless, I am confident that the situation will not become so serious as to force any basic changes in the diplomatic and political posture of this country."

The Socialists and the Communists openly stand for the recognition of Communist China by Japan. But diplomatic recognition of the Peking government by Tokyo seems to be still distant. Japan cannot possibly ignore the American sentiments. Moreover, the Tokyo-Taiwan (Formosa) diplomatic relation is another formidable obstacle. Japan has concluded a peace treaty with Taiwan and she has also a very substantial trade with the latter. The Socialists stand for the admission of Communist China to the membership of the United Nations.

The domestic policy of the Socialist Party seeks to emphasize nationalization of basic industries, stabilization of prices, improvements in social insurance and old age pension schemes and elimination of disparities in income and standards of living in rural and urban areas. The Communist Party pleads for the betterment of the economic conditions of the poorer sections of the Japanese population. The Democratic Socialist Party seeks "to increase the income of the working public and reform the economic system to prevent large enterprises and millionaires from getting the lion's share. Special emphasis to be placed on boosting backward industries (agriculture, fisheries and forestry) as well as smaller enterprises and perfecting the social insurance system."[1]

In the field of international relations the Komeito believes that Japan should take the initiative in peace. Chairman Takeiri has said: "Japan must contribute to the achievement of a warless, peaceful world through realistic, steady efforts under a lofty ideal. This is exactly what the Asian nations strongly expect of Japan in view of this country's geographical, cultural and economic conditions. We must be fully conscious that such efforts will also aid the firm establishment of peace and security for Japan."

His party favours a phasing out of the Japan-U.S. Security Treaty and to maintain the neutrality essential for the policy of non-alignment and non-armament. It has put forward the idea of establishing a regional Asian United Nations headquarters in Japan. The Komeito seeks the establishment of friendly relations with China and to settle the question of the Kurile islands with the Soviet Union.

Takeiri says: "We are determined to assert the Komeito's position clearly to all nations both in the Communist bloc and the free world in an effort to deepen mutual understanding and international friendship."[2]

If the foreign policy of the Komei Party is idealistic then no less is its domestic policy which recognizes those problems which "plague industrial society: air and water pollution, crowded housing and transportation conditions, and the high cost of living." However, its policy statements, both foreign and domestic, have proved their voter appeal.

In the last General Election (1969) the Komeito has firmly established itself as the third largest party in the Lower House of the national legislature. But it is widely criticized for mixing politics with religion. However, one of the reorganizational moves taken by the party after the election seeks to separate it from Sokagakkai's Buddhist movement. The resignation of

[1] *The Japan Times*, May 7, 1959. Quoted by Burks, p. 87.
[2] Quoted by Jean Pearce, *Amrita Bazar Patrika*, February 2, 1970.

Yoshikatsu Takeiri, Chairman of the Komeito, and Jun'ye Yano, Secretary-General, from their executive positions with the Sokagakkai is indicative of this move.

Sivapali Wickremansinghe refers to one beneficial effect of the existence of a politico-religious party. He observes: "Whether Komeito's and Sokagakkai's efforts to bring about a 'political and religious revolution' will be successful is highly uncertain. But the existence of the party certainly has one beneficial effect: it keeps the other parties on their toes and gives them something to think about."

CHAPTER 10

Local Self-Government

Democracy is said to have an educative value. But the educative value of democracy depends very largely upon the nature and spirit of its local institutions.

—W. B. Munro

LOCAL SELF-GOVERNING institutions are the training centres of democracy. They provide opportunities to the local inhabitants to participate in the management of local affairs and prepare themselves to assume larger responsibilities of national administration. But Japan had no tradition of local self-government. Under the Meiji Constitution administration was thoroughly centralized. The principle of local autonomy was unknown. As McNelly observes: "Centralization and bureaucracy rather than local autonomy and democracy were the prevailing principles of local government in pre-war Japan."[1]

Small area of the country, similarities of language and religion facilitated centralized control over the prefectures which were established after the Meiji Restoration. Moreover, regional economic disparities were not so sharp as to necessitate a large measure of regional autonomy. Over and above were die-hard nationalism and the Emperor system which glorified national unity and centralized government over local autonomy.

The American Occupation authorities were, however, determined to dismantle the authoritarian structure. Decentralization and democratization of Japan were sought to be achieved through the granting of extensive rights to the local self-governing institutions. The new Constitution accordingly accepts the principle of local autonomy.

[1] McNelly, *Contemporary Government of Japan*, p. 155.

Article 92 of the Constitution says: "Regulations concerning organization and operations of local public entities shall be fixed by law in accordance with the principle of local autonomy."

"The local public entities establish assemblies as their deliberative organs in accordance with law. The chief executive officers of all local public entities, the members of their assemblies and other local officials are elected by direct popular vote within their several communities."[1]

Article 95 of the Constitution says that a special law applicable only to one local public entity cannot be enacted by the Diet without the consent of the majority of the voters of the local public entity concerned obtained in accordance with law. This Article may be interpreted as a limitation upon the authority of the Diet to legislate for the local bodies and at the same time as giving emphasis on the autonomy of the local units.

The local government in Japan is organized into 46 prefectures which include the Tokyo metropolis, two urban prefectures (Kyoto and Osaka), 42 rural prefectures and the Hokkaido district. A prefecture is the highest unit of local government in Japan the territory of which is then sub-divided into cities, towns and villages. These are the lowest units of local self-government except three large cities which are designated as special cities. The number of the sub-divisions as it stood in 1965 is as follows: 561 cities, 2,007 towns and 808 villages.

In each prefecture there is a governor who is its chief executive officer and a single-house assembly which is its deliberative organ. The governor is elected for a term of 4 years by the voters of the prefecture and may be recalled by them. He is also subject to the vote of no confidence of the prefectural assembly.

The members of the prefectural assembly are also elected for 4 years by the voters of the prefecture and may be recalled by them. The voters may also demand a dissolution of the entire assembly. The size of the prefectural assembly varies from 40 to 120 members depending on the population of the prefecture.

[1] Art. 93

Both the governor and the assembly are subject to the control of the local electorate. If one-third of the voters in a prefecture demand the removal of the governor and this demand is supported by a majority in a recall election, the governor must resign. Similarly one-third of the voters may demand the dissolution of the entire assembly or the resignation of an individual member. If this demand is supported by a majority of the voters the entire assembly or the individual member, as the case may be, must resign.

The relationship between the governor and the prefectural assembly resembles the executive-legislative relationship in a parliamentary system of government. The governor may veto a measure passed by the prefectural assembly which the latter may overcome by a two-thirds majority. Upon a no-confidence motion of the assembly the governor must either resign or dissolve the assembly. In the event of a dissolution a new assembly has to be elected. If the new assembly also adopts the no-confidence resolution immediately after its reconstitution the governor must resign.

The subjects over which the legislative authority of the local assembly extends are enumerated in the Local Autonomy Law. These include the budget of prefectural government, acquisition, management and disposal of its property, levy and collection of local taxes. Article 94 of the Constitution says: Local public entities shall have the right to manage their property, affairs and administration to enact their own regulations within law.

Administration in cities, towns and villages is similar to that of the prefectures. Each city, town and village has its own mayor and a single House. Mayor like the governor of the prefecture is elected for 4 years by the voters of the local unit and may be recalled by them and is also subject to the vote of no confidence of the local council. Like the members of the prefectural assembly the members of the local council are also elected for a term of 4 years by the local electorate and may be recalled by them. A local council is also subject to dissolution by the mayor or on a demand of the voters themselves. The relation between the mayor and the local council is identical to that of the governor and the prefectural assembly.

The governor of a prefecture while acting as an organ of the national government is subject to the control of the national Autonomy Ministry and in extreme cases of failure or refusal to enforce a national law the governor may be removed from office by the Prime Minister. A mayor while acting as an organ of the national government is subject to a dual control, that of the competent Cabinet Minister and the governor of the prefecture and for his failure or refusal to enforce a national law or a prefectural by-law he may be removed from office by the governor of the prefecture.

To be a governor or a mayor a person must be a Japanese national and must be at least 30 years of age for governorship and 25 years for mayoralty. A governor or a mayor may not be a member of the Diet or of the local assembly at the same time. Candidates for the local assembly must be at least 25 years of age. A candidate for governorship or mayoralty is not required to reside in the locality in which he is seeking office. But the candidates for election to the local councils must be residents of the locality—city, town or the village—although this is not required of the candidates for prefectural assemblies.

The local public entities in Japan perform all those functions which are incidental to local self-governing units. These are: maintenance of public order, public health, safety of the local inhabitants, establishment and management of parks, playgrounds, canals, drainage, waterways, water plants, sewerage systems, electric plants, gas plants, public transportation systems, docks, piers, warehouses, schools, libraries, museums, hospitals, asylums for the aged, jails, crematories, cemeteries, disaster relief, land reclamation, identification and registration of local inhabitants. It is clear, therefore, that the powers given to the local public entities are extensive in scope.

Although the local public entities are under the Constitution legally autonomous, in practice they are not. The Constitution has not enumerated the powers and functions of the local self-governing units with the result that they exercise only those powers and discharge those functions which are delegated to them by the national Diet. The Constitution has authorized the local units to manage their affairs and to make their own regulations. In practice, they administer the policies of the national government at the local level.

Moreover, the local public entities are not independent self-supporting economic units. Their financial foundation is very weak. Although the local entities have power to levy and collect local taxes, actual collection is highly inadequate. The result is, they are sustained largely by national government subsidies and grants-in-aid. This economic dependency compromises to a great extent the principle of local autonomy. As Nakai Mitsuji has observed: One of the basic problems is financial stringency which plagues many prefectures and cities—much to the detriment of the wholesome growth of local autonomy.[1]

Not only local finance, local police and even education are controlled by the national government while the Autonomy Ministry has the general power of supervision over the local governments. Thus the original policy of decentralization is giving way to at least a partial recentralization of government in Japan.

---

[1] "Local Autonomy", *The Japan Times*, December 10, 1958. Quoted by Burks, p. 217.

Chronological Outlines 1868-1968

Chronological outline of some of the most important events in the history of modern Japan during the last 100 years.

1867   *Edo Period.* (1603-1867) The 15th Tokugawa Shogun returned national rule to the Imperial Throne, ending the Tokugawa Shogunate and the rule of warrior government which had started towards the end of the 13th century.

1868   *Meiji Period.* (1868-1912) With the restoration of Imperial rule Emperor Meiji issued an order establishing a new officialdom and proclaiming the direct rule of the Throne in every line of national government.

—Emperor Meiji issued a five-point oath laying emphasis on respecting public opinion, developing relations with foreign countries and seeking knowledge far and wide.

—Edo was renamed Tokyo, and fixed as the national capital.

—Emperor Meiji arrived in Tokyo to establish the Imperial Residence in the new capital.

1869   The feudal lords returned their domains and people to the Throne.

1870   The feudal caste system of warrior, farmer, artisan and merchant was abolished.

1875   The Meiji Government established the Supreme Court, thereby setting up the new judicial system.

1889   The Meiji Constitution was promulgated and limited suffrage introduced.

1890   The first session of the national parliament was inaugurated, giving the nation the form of constitutional government.

1894   The Treaty of Commerce and Navigation with Great Britain was signed. Thus was brought to a conclusion the lengthy series of negotiations for the revision of the unequal treaties entered into by the Tokugawa Shogunate.

—Conflicting interests in Korea led to the outbreak of the Sino-Japanese war.

1895   The war with China ended in victory for Japan.

1902   The Anglo-Japanese Alliance was concluded.

1904   Opposing the advance of Russian influence into Korea, Japan declared war on Russia.

1905   Japan emerged victorious in the Russo-Japanese war.

1910   Japan annexed Korea.

1912   Emperor Meiji passed away.

1912   *Taisho Period* (1912-1926). Emperor Taisho acceded to the Imperial Throne.

1914   World War I broke out and Japan entered the war on the side of the Allies.

1919   The Versailles Treaty was concluded, with Japan as one of the Allied signatories.

1920   Japan joined the League of Nations.

1921   Japan participated in the disarmament conference at Washington, D.C.

1925   Universal suffrage for adult males was adopted.

1926   *Showa Period* (1926). Emperor Taisho passed away and was succeeded by the present Emperor. The name Showa was given to the new era.

1930   Japan participated in the London Disarmament Conference.

1931   The Manchurian Incident, which led to the Japanese domination of Manchuria, broke out.

1933   Japan withdrew from the League of Nations, in protest against the League's opposition to Japan's action in Manchuria.

1937   With increasing military interference and control in politics, Japan started large-scale military operations in China.

1940   Japan concluded an alliance with Germany and Italy, making her one of the Rome-Berlin-Tokyo Axis Powers.

1941   Japan launched hostilities against the United States and Great Britain, thus entering World War II.

1945   Japan surrendered unconditionally to the Allied Powers on the basis of the Potsdam Declaration. Japanese military forces were demobilized, and a programme of thorough democratization was instituted.

1946   The new Constitution was adopted, and universal suffrage was extended to women.

1950   With the outbreak of hostilities in Korea, the Supreme Commander of the Allied Powers in Tokyo instructed the Japanese Government to set up a National Police Reserve and to increase the strength of the Maritime Safety Agency, the embryo of the present Self-Defence Forces.

1951   Japan signed a peace treaty at San Francisco with the United States and almost all of the other Allied Powers.

    —The Mutual Security Treaty between Japan and the United States was concluded.

1952   The San Francisco Peace Treaty came into force, and the Allied occupation ended, restoring full independence to Japan.

    —A separate peace treaty was concluded with the Republic of China.

1956   Japan's diplomatic relations with the Soviet Union were restored, with a Joint Declaration terminating the state of war between the two nations.

    —Japan was admitted to the membership in the United Nations.

1965   The Treaty on Basic Relations between Japan and the Republic of Korea was signed.

1968   Ceremonies for the Meiji Centenary, marking the 100th anniversary of the start of the Meiji Era, were held throughout the country.

APPENDIX–2

National Governmental Structure

EMPEROR

DIET	CABINET	COURTS
House of Representatives	Board of Audit	Supreme Court
House of Councillors	Prime Minister's Office	High Courts (8)
Judge Impeachment Court	Ministry of Justice	District Courts (49)
Judge Indictment Committee	Ministry of Foreign Affairs	Family Courts (49)
National Diet Library	Ministry of Finance	Summary Courts (570)
	Ministry of Education	Non-Indictment Review Committees (204)
	Ministry of Health and Welfare	
	Ministry of Agriculture and Forestry	
	Ministry of International Trade and Industry	
	Ministry of Transport	
	Ministry of Posts and Telecommunications	
	Ministry of Labour	
	Ministry of Construction	
	Ministry of Home Affairs	

Board of Audit Executive Office 1,209	*Cabinet*	
Secretariat	Cabinet Secretariat (79)	National Personnel Authority Executive Office (724)
First Bureau	Cabinet Legislation Bureau (74)	Bureau of Administrative Services
Second Bureau	First Department	Bureau of Recruitment
Third Bureau	Second Department	Bureau of Compensation
Fourth Bureau	Third Department	Bureau of Equity
Fifth Bureau	Fourth Department	Bureau of Employee Relations
	Office of the Director-General	Institute of Public Administration
	National Defence Council (21)	Regional Offices (8)

National Administrative Organs

Office on the Ministerial Level or Ministry	Commission	Agency
Prime Minister's Office	Fair Trade Commission	Imperial Household Agency
	National Public Safety Commission	Administrative Management Agency
	Land Coordination Commission	Hokkaido Development Agency
	National Capital Region Development Commission	Defence Agency
		Economic Planning Agency
		Science and Technology Agency
		Defence Facilities Administration Agency
Ministry of Justice	Administration Commission of National Bar Examination	Public Security Investigation Agency
	Public Safety Investigation Commission	
Ministry of Foreign Affairs		
Ministry of Finance		Tax Administration Agency
Ministry of Education		Culture Affairs Agency
Ministry of Health and Welfare		Social Insurance Agency
Ministry of Agriculture and Forestry		Food Agency
		Forestry Agency
		Fisheries Agency
Ministry of International Trade and Industry		Patent Office
		Smaller Enterprises Agency
Ministry of Transport	Central Labour Relations Commission for Seafares	Maritime Safety Agency
		Marine Accidents Inquiry Agency
		Meteorological Agency

Ministry of Posts and
   Telecommunications

Ministry of Labour   Central Labour Relations
                      Commission
                      Public Corporation and
                      National Enterprise
                      Labour Relations
                      Commission

Ministry of Construction

Ministry of Home Affairs   Fire Defence Agency

Ministry of Finance

Ministry of Agriculture
   and Forestry

Ministry of International
   Trade and Industry

Party Positions in the Diet as on January 29, 1967

Name of the Parties	House of Representatives (Lower House)	House of Councillors (Upper House)
Liberal Democratic Party	277	140
Socialist Party	140	73
Democratic Socialist Party	30	6
Communist Party	5	4
Komei Party	25	20
Independents	9	5
Vacant Seats	0	2
Total	486	250

Distribution of Lower House Seats by Party as of January 6, 1970*

Liberal Democratic Party	300
Socialist Party	90
Komei Party	47
Democratic Socialist Party	32
Communist Party	14
Splinter Parties	0
Independents	3
Total	486

*General Election held on December 27, 1969/New Sato Cabinet formed on January 14, 1970.

The Constitution of Japan

We, the Japanese people, acting through our duly elected representatives in the National Diet, determined that we shall secure for ourselves and our posterity the fruits of peaceful cooperation with all nations and the blessings of liberty throughout this land, and resolved that never again shall we be visited with the horrors of war through the action of government, do proclaim that sovereign power resides with the people and do firmly establish this Constitution. Government is a sacred trust of the people, the authority for which is derived from the people, the powers of which are exercised by the representatives of the people, and the benefits of which are enjoyed by the people. This is a universal principle of mankind upon which this Constitution is founded. We reject and revoke all constitutions, laws, ordinances and rescripts in conflict herewith.

We, the Japanese people, desire peace for all time and are deeply conscious of the high ideals controlling human relationship, and we have determined to preserve our security and existence, trusting in the justice and faith of the peace-loving peoples of the world. We desire to occupy an honoured place in an international society striving for the preservation of peace, and the banishment of tyranny and slavery, oppression and intolerance for all time from the earth. We recognize that all peoples of the world have the right to live in peace, free from fear and want.

We believe that no nation is responsible to itself alone, but that laws of political morality are universal; and that obedience to such laws is incumbent upon all nations who would sustain their own sovereignty and justify their sovereign relationship with other nations.

We, the Japanese people, pledge our national honour to accomplish these high ideals and purposes with all our resources.

Chapter I. The Emperor

ARTICLE 1. The Emperor shall be the symbol of the state and of the unity of the people, deriving his position from the will of the people with whom resides sovereign power.

ARTICLE 2. The Imperial Throne shall be dynastic and succeeded to in accordance with the Imperial House Law passed by the Diet.

ARTICLE 3. The advice and approval of the Cabinet shall be required for all acts of the Emperor in matters of state, and the Cabinet shall be responsible therefor.

ARTICLE 4. The Emperor shall perform only such acts in matters of state as are provided for in this Constitution and he shall not have powers related to government.

The Emperor may delegate the performance of his acts in matters of state as may be provided by law.

ARTICLE 5. When, in accordance with the Imperial House Law, a Regency is established, the Regent shall perform his acts in matters of state in the Emperor's name. In this case, paragraph one of the preceding Article will be applicable.

ARTICLE 6. The Emperor shall appoint the Prime Minister as designated by the Diet.

The Emperor shall appoint the Chief Judge of the Supreme Court as designated by the Cabinet.

ARTICLE 7. The Emperor, with the advice and approval of the Cabinet, shall perform the following acts in matters of state on behalf of the people:

Promulgation of amendments of the Constitution, laws, Cabinet orders and treaties.

Convocation of the Diet.

Dissolution of the House of Representatives.

Proclamation of general election of members of the Diet.

Attestation of the appointment and dismissal of Ministers of State and other officials as provided for by law, and of full powers and credentials of Ambassadors and Ministers.

Attestation of general and special amnesty, commutation of punishment, reprieve, and restoration of rights.

Awarding of honours.

Attestation of instruments of ratification and other diplomatic documents as provided for by law.

Receiving foreign Ambassadors and Ministers.

Performance of ceremonial functions.

ARTICLE 8. No property can be given to, or received by, the Imperial House, nor can any gifts be made therefrom, without the authorization of the Diet.

Chapter II. Renunciation of War

ARTICLE 9. Aspiring sincerely to an international peace based on justice and order, the Japanese people forever renounce war as a sovereign right of the nation and the threat or use of force as means of settling international disputes.

In order to accomplish the aim of the preceding paragraph, land, sea, and air forces, as well as other war potential, will never be maintained. The right of belligerency of the state will not be recognized.

Chapter III. Rights and Duties of the People

ARTICLE 10. The conditions necessary for being a Japanese national shall be determined by law.

ARTICLE 11. The people shall not be prevented from enjoying any of the fundamental human rights. These fundamental human rights guaranteed to the people by this Constitution shall be conferred upon the people of this and future generations as eternal and inviolate rights.

ARTICLE 12. The freedom and rights guaranteed to the people by this Constitution shall be maintained by the constant endeavour of the people, who shall refrain from any abuse of these freedoms and rights and shall always be responsible for utilizing them for the public welfare.

ARTICLE 13. All of the people shall be respected as individuals. Their right to life, liberty, and the pursuit of happiness shall, to the extent that it does not interfere with the public welfare, be the supreme consideration in legislation and in other governmental affairs.

ARTICLE 14. All of the people are equal under the law and there shall be no discrimination in political, economic or social relations because of race, creed, sex, social status or family origin.

Peers and peerage shall not be recognized.

No privilege shall accompany any award of honour, decoration or any distinction, nor shall any such award be valid beyond the lifetime of the individual who now holds or hereafter may receive it.

ARTICLE 15. The people have the inalienable right to choose their public officials and to dismiss them.

All public officials are servants of the whole community and not of any group thereof.

Universal adult suffrage is guaranteed with regard to the election of public officials.

In all elections, secrecy of the ballot shall not be violated. A voter shall not be answerable, publicly or privately, for the choice he has made.

ARTICLE 16. Every person shall have the right of peaceful petition for the redress of damage, for the removal of public officials, for the enactment, repeal or amendment of laws, ordinances or regulations and for other matters, nor shall any person be in any way discriminated against for sponsoring such a petition.

ARTICLE 17. Every person may sue for redress as provided by law from the state or public entity, in case he has suffered damage through illegal act of any public official.

ARTICLE 18. No person shall be held in bondage of any kind. Involuntary servitude, except as punishment for crime, is prohibited.

ARTICLE 19. Freedom of thought and conscience shall not be violated.

ARTICLE 20. Freedom of religion is guaranteed to all. No religious organization shall receive any privileges from the state, nor exercise any political authority.

No person shall be compelled to take part in any religious act, celebration, rite or practice.

The state and its organs shall refrain from religious education or any other religious activity.

ARTICLE 21. Freedom of assembly and association as well as speech, Press and all other forms of expression are guaranteed.

No censorship shall be maintained, nor shall the secrecy of any means of communication be violated.

ARTICLE 22. Every person shall have freedom to choose and change his residence and to choose his occupation to the extent that it does not interfere with the public welfare.

Freedom of all persons to move to a foreign country and to divest themselves of their nationality shall be inviolate.

ARTICLE 23. Academic freedom is guaranteed.

ARTICLE 24. Marriage shall be based only on the mutual consent of both sexes and it shall be maintained through mutual co-operation with the equal rights of husband and wife as a basis.

With regard to choice of spouse, property rights, inheritance, choice of domicile, divorce and other matters pertaining to marriage and the family, laws shall be enacted from the standpoint of individual dignity and the essential equality of the sexes.

ARTICLE 25. All people shall have the right to maintain the minimum standards of wholesome and cultured living.

In all spheres of life, the state shall use its endeavours for the promotion and extension of social welfare and security, and of public health.

ARTICLE 26. All people shall have the right to receive an equal education correspondent to their ability, as provided by law.

All people shall be obligated to have all boys and girls under their protection receive ordinary education as provided for by law. Such compulsory education shall be free.

ARTICLE 27. All people shall have the right and the obligation to work.

Standards for wages, hours, rest and other working conditions shall be fixed by law.

Children shall not be exploited.

ARTICLE 28. The right of workers to organize and to bargain and act collectively is guaranteed.

ARTICLE 29. The right to own or to hold property is inviolable.

Property rights shall be defined by law, in conformity with the public welfare.

Private property may be taken for public use upon just compensation therefor.

ARTICLE 30. The people shall be liable to taxation as provided by law.

ARTICLE 31. No person shall be deprived of life or liberty, nor shall any other criminal penalty be imposed, except according to procedure established by law.

ARTICLE 32. No person shall be denied the right of access to the courts.

ARTICLE 33. No person shall be apprehended except upon warrant issued by a competent judicial officer which specifies the offence with which the person is charged, unless he is apprehended, the offence being committed.

ARTICLE 34. No person shall be arrested or detained without being at once informed of the charges against him or without the immediate privilege of counsel; nor shall he be detained without adequate cause; and upon demand of any person such cause must be immediately shown in open court in his presence and the presence of his counsel.

ARTICLE 35. The right of all persons to be secure in their homes, papers and effects against entries, searches and seizures shall not be impaired except upon warrant issued for adequate cause and particularly describing the place to be searched and things to be seized, or except as provided by Article 33.

Each search or seizure shall be made upon separate warrant issued by a competent judicial officer.

ARTICLE 36. The infliction of torture by any public officer and cruel punishments are absolutely forbidden.

ARTICLE 37. In all criminal cases the accused shall enjoy the right to a speedy and public trial by an impartial tribunal.

He shall be permitted full opportunity to examine all witnesses, and he shall have the right of compulsory process for obtaining witnesses on his behalf at public expense.

At all times the accused shall have the assistance of competent counsel who shall, if the accused is unable to secure the same by his own efforts, be assigned to his use by the state.

ARTICLE 38. No person shall be compelled to testify against himself.

Confession made under compulsion, torture or threat, or after prolonged arrest or detention shall not be admitted in evidence.

No person shall be convicted or punished in cases where the only proof against him is his own confession.

ARTICLE 39. No person shall be held criminally liable for an act which was lawful at the time it was committed, or of which he has been acquitted, nor shall he be placed in double jeopardy.

ARTICLE 40. Any person, in case he is acquitted after he has been arrested or detained, may sue the state for redress as provided by law.

Chapter IV. The Diet

ARTICLE 41. The Diet shall be the highest organ of state power, and shall be the sole law-making organ of the state.

ARTICLE 42. The Diet shall consist of two Houses, namely the House of Representatives and the House of Councillors.

ARTICLE 43. Both Houses shall consist of elected members, representative of all the people.

The number of the members of each House shall be fixed by law.

ARTICLE 44. The qualifications of members of both Houses and their electors shall be fixed by law. However, there shall be no discrimination because of race, creed, sex, social status, family origin, education, property or income.

ARTICLE 45. The term of office of members of the House of Representatives shall be four years. However, the term shall be terminated before the full term is up in case the House of Representatives is dissolved.

ARTICLE 46. The term of office of members of the House of Councillors shall be six years, and election for half the members shall take place every three years.

ARTICLE 47. Electoral districts, method of voting and other matters pertaining to the method of election of members of both Houses shall be fixed by law.

ARTICLE 48. No person shall be permitted to be a member of both Houses simultaneously.

ARTICLE 49. Members of both Houses shall receive appropriate annual payment from the national treasury in accordance with law.

ARTICLE 50. Except in cases provided by law, members of both Houses shall be exempt from apprehension while the Diet is in session, and any members apprehended before the opening of the session shall be freed during the term of the session upon demand of the House.

ARTICLE 51. Members of both Houses shall not be held liable outside the House for speeches, debates or votes cast inside the House.

ARTICLE 52. An ordinary session of the Diet shall be convoked once per year.

ARTICLE 53. The Cabinet may determine to convoke extraordinary sessions of the Diet. When a quarter or more of the total members of either House makes the demand, the Cabinet must determine on such convocation.

ARTICLE 54. When the House of Representatives is dissolved, there must be a general election of members of the House of Representatives within forty (40) days from the date of dissolution, and the Diet must be convoked within thirty (30) days from the date of the election.

When the House of Representatives is dissolved, the House of Councillors is closed at the same time. However, the Cabinet may in time of national emergency convoke the House of Councillors in emergency session.

Measures taken at such session as mentioned in the proviso of the preceding paragraph shall be provisional and shall become null and void unless agreed to by the House of Representatives within a period of ten (10) days after the opening of the next session of the Diet.

ARTICLE 55. Each House shall judge disputes related to qualifications of its members. However, in order to deny a seat to any member, it is necessary to pass a resolution by a majority of two-thirds or more of the members present.

ARTICLE 56. Business cannot be transacted in either House unless one-third or more of total membership is present.

All matters shall be decided, in each House, by a majority of those present, except as elsewhere provided in the Constitution, and in case of a tie, the presiding officer shall decide the issue.

ARTICLE 57. Deliberation in each House shall be public However, a secret meeting may be held where a majority of two-thirds or more of those members prneset passes a resolution therefor.

Each House shall keep a record of proceedings. This record shall be published and given general circulation, excepting such parts of proceedings of secret session as may be deemed to require secrecy.

Upon demand of one-fifth or more of the members present, votes of the members on any matter shall be recorded in the minutes.

ARTICLE 58. Each House shall select its own president and other officials.

Each House shall establish its rules pertaining to meetings, proceedings and internal discipline, and may punish members for disorderly conduct. However, in order to expel a member, a majority of two-thirds or more of those members present must pass a resolution thereon.

ARTICLE 59. A Bill becomes a law on passage by both Houses, except as otherwise provided by the Constitution.

A Bill which is passed by the House of Representatives, and upon which the House of Councillors makes a decision different from that of the House of Representatives, becomes a law when passed a second time by the House of Representatives by a majority of two-thirds or more of the members present.

The provision of the preceding paragraph does not preclude the House of Representatives from calling for the meeting of a joint committee of both Houses. provided for by law.

Failure by the House of Councillors to take final action within sixty (60) days after receipt of a Bill passed by the House of Representatives, time in recess excepted, may be determined by the House of Representatives to constitute a rejection of the said Bill by the House of Councillors.

ARTICLE 60. The budget must first be submitted to the House of Representatives.

Upon consideration of the budget, when the House of Councillors makes a decision different from that of the House of Representatives, and when no agreement can be reached even through a joint committee of both Houses, provided for by law, or in the case of failure by the House of Councillors to take final action within thirty (30) days, the period of recess excluded, after the receipt of the budget passed by the House of Representatives, the decision of the House of Representatives shall be the decision of the Diet.

ARTICLE 61. The second paragraph of the preceding Article applies also to the Diet approval required for the conclusion of treaties.

ARTICLE 62. Each House may conduct investigations in relation to government, and may demand the presence and testimony of witnesses, and the production of records.

ARTICLE 63. The Prime Minister and other Ministers of State may, at any time, appear in either House for the purpose of speaking on Bills, regardless of whether they are members of the House or not. They must appear when their presence is required in order to give answers or explanations.

ARTICLE 64. The Diet shall set up an impeachment court from among the members of both Houses for the purpose of trying those judges against whom removal proceedings have been instituted.

Matters relating to impeachment shall be provided by law.

Chapter V. The Cabinet

ARTICLE 65. Executive power shall be vested in the Cabinet.

ARTICLE 66. The Cabinet shall consist of the Prime Minister, who shall be its head, and other Ministers of State, as provided for by law.

The Prime Minister and other Ministers of State must be civilians.

The Cabinet in the exercise of executive power, shall be collectively responsible to the Diet.

ARTICLE 67. The Prime Minister shall be designated from among the members of the Diet by a resolution of the Diet. This designation shall precede all other business.

If the House of Representatives and the House of Councillors disagree and if no agreement can be reached even through a joint committee of both Houses, provided for by law, or the House of Councillors fails to make designation within ten (10) days, exclusive of the period of recess, after the House of Representatives has made designation, the decision of the House of Representatives shall be the decision of the Diet.

ARTICLE 68. The Prime Minister shall appoint the Ministers of State. However, a majority of their number must be chosen from among the members of the Diet.

The Prime Minister may remove the Ministers of State as he chooses.

ARTICLE 69. If the House of Representatives passes a non-confidence resolution, or rejects a confidence resolution, the Cabinet shall resign en masse, unless the House of Representatives is dissolved within ten (10) days.

ARTICLE 70. When there is a vacancy in the post of Prime Minister, or upon the first convocation of the Diet after a general election of members of the House of Representatives, the Cabinet shall resign en masse.

ARTICLE 71. In the cases mentioned in the two preceding Articles, the Cabinet shall continue its functions until the time when a new Prime Minister is appointed.

ARTICLE 72. The Prime Minister, representing the Cabinet, submits Bills, reports on general national affairs and foreign relations to the Diet and exercises control and supervision over various administrative branches.

ARTICLE 73. The Cabinet, in addition to other general administrative functions, shall perform the following functions:

Administer the law faithfully; conduct affairs of state.

Manage foreign affairs.

Conclude treaties. However, it shall obtain prior or, depending on circumstances, subsequent approval of the Diet.

Administer the civil service, in accordance with standards established by law.

Prepare the budget, and present it to the Diet.

Enact Cabinet orders in order to execute the provisions of this Constitution and of the law.

However, it cannot include penal provisions in such Cabinet orders unless authorized by such law.

Decide on general amnesty, special amnesty, commutation of punishment, reprieve, and restoration of rights.

ARTICLE 74. All laws and Cabinet orders shall be signed by the competent Minister of State and countersigned by the Prime Minister.

ARTICLE 75. The Ministers of State, during their tenure of office, shall not be subject to legal action without the consent of the Prime Minister. However, the right to take that action is not impaired hereby.

Chapter VI. Judiciary

ARTICLE 76. The whole judicial power is vested in a Supreme Court and in such inferior courts as are established by law.

No extraordinary tribunal shall be established, nor shall any organ or agency of the Executive be given final judicial power.

All judges shall be independent in the exercise of their conscience and shall be bound only by this Constitution and the laws.

ARTICLE 77. The Supreme Court is vested with the rule-making power under which it determines the rules of procedure and of practice, and of matters relating to attorneys, the internal discipline of the courts and the administration of judicial affairs.

Public procurators shall be subject to the rule-making power of the Supreme Court.

The Supreme Court may delegate the power to make rules for inferior courts to such courts.

ARTICLE 78. Judges shall not be removed except by public impeachment unless judicially declared mentally or physically incompetent to perform official duties. No disciplinary action against judges shall be administered by any executive organ or agency.

ARTICLE 79. The Supreme Court shall consist of a Chief Judge and such number of judges as may be determined by law; all such judges excepting the Chief Judge shall be appointed by the Cabinet.

The appointment of the judges of the Supreme Court shall be reviewed by the people at the first general election of members of the House of Representatives following their appointment, and shall be reviewed again at the first general election of members of the House of Representatives after a lapse of ten (10) years, and in the same manner thereafter.

In cases mentioned in the foregoing paragraph, when the majority of the voters favours the dismissal of a judge, he shall be dismissed.

Matters pertaining to review shall be prescribed by law.

The Judges of the Supreme Court shall be retired upon the attainment of the age as fixed by law.

All such judges shall receive, at regular stated intervals, adequate compensation which shall not be decreased during their terms of office.

ARTICLE 80. The judges of the inferior courts shall be appointed by the Cabinet from a list of persons nominated by the Supreme Court. All such judges shall hold office for a term of ten (10) years with privilege of reappointment, provided that they shall be retired upon the attainment of the age as fixed by law.

The judges of the inferior courts shall receive, at regular stated intervals, adequate compensation which shall not be decreased during their terms of office.

ARTICLE 81. The Supreme Court is the court of last resort with power to determine the constitutionality of any law, order, regulation or official act.

ARTICLE 82. Trials shall be conducted and judgment declared publicly. Where a court unanimously determines publicity to be dangerous to public order or morals, a trial may be conducted privately, but trials of political offences, offences involving the Press or cases wherein the rights of people as guaranteed in Chapter III of this Constitution are in question shall always be conducted publicly.

Chapter VII. Finance

ARTICLE 83. The power to administer national finances shall be exercised as the Diet shall determine.

ARTICLE 84. No new taxes shall be imposed or existing ones modified except by law or under such conditions as law may prescribe.

ARTICLE 85. No money shall be expended, nor shall the state obligate itself, except as authorized by the Diet.

ARTICLE 86. The Cabinet shall prepare and submit to the Diet for its consideration and decision a budget for each fiscal year.

ARTICLE 87. In order to provide for unforeseen deficiencies in the budget, a reserve fund may be authorized by the Diet to be expended upon the responsibility of the Cabinet.

The Cabinet must get subsequent approval of the Diet for all payments from the reserve fund.

ARTICLE 88. All property of the Imperial Household shall belong to the state. All expenses of the Imperial Household shall be appropriated by the Diet in the budget.

ARTICLE 89. No public money or other property shall be expended or appropriated for the use, benefit or maintenance of any religious institution or association, or for any charitable, educational or benevolent enterprises not under the control of public authority.

ARTICLE 90. Final accounts of the expenditures and revenues of the state shall be audited annually by a Board of Audit and submitted by the Cabinet to the Diet, together with the statement of audit during the fiscal year immediately following the period covered.

The organization and competency of the Board of Audit shall be determined by law.

ARTICLE 91. At regular intervals and at least annually the Cabinet shall report to the Diet and the people on the state of national finances.

Chapter VIII. Local Self-Government

ARTICLE 92. Regulations concerning organization and operations of local public entities shall be fixed by law in accordance with the principle of local autonomy.

ARTICLE 93. The local public entities shall establish assemblies as their deliberative organs, in accordance with law.

The chief executive officers of all local public entities, the members of their assemblies, and such other local officials as may be determined by law shall be elected by direct popular vote within their several communities.

ARTICLE 94. Local public entities shall have the right to manage their property, affairs and administration and to enact their own regulations within law.

ARTICLE 95. A special law applicable only to one local

public entity cannot be enacted by the Diet without the consent of the majority of the voters of the local public entity concerned, obtained in accordance with law.

Chapter IX. Amendments

ARTICLE 96. Amendments to this Constitution shall be initiated by the Diet, through a concurring vote of two-thirds or more of all the members of each House and shall thereupon be submitted to the people for ratification, which shall require the affirmative vote of a majority of all votes cast thereon, at a special referendum or at such election as the Diet shall specify.

Amendments when so ratified shall immediately be promulgated by the Emperor in the name of the people, as an integral part of this Constitution.

Chapter X. Supreme Law

ARTICLE 97. The fundamental human rights by this Constitution guaranteed to the people of Japan are fruits of the age-old struggle of man to be free; they have survived the many exacting tests for durability and are conferred upon this and future generations in trust, to be held for all time inviolate.

ARTICLE 98. This Constitution shall be the supreme law of the nation and no law, ordinance, imperial rescript or other act of government, or part thereof, contrary to the provisions hereof, shall have legal force or validity.

The treaties concluded by Japan and established laws of nations shall be faithfully observed.

ARTICLE 99. The Emperor or the Regent as well as Ministers of State, members of the Diet, judges, and all other public officials have the obligation to respect and uphold this Constitution.

Chapter XI. Supplementary Provisions

ARTICLE 100. This Constitution shall be enforced as from the day when the period of six months will have elapsed counting from the day of its promulgation.

The enactment of laws necessary for the enforcement of this Constitution, the election of members of the House of Councillors, and the procedure for the convocation of the Diet and other preparatory procedures necessary for the enforcement of this Constitution, may be executed before the day prescribed in the preceding paragraph.

ARTICLE 101. If the House of Councillors is not constituted before the effective date of this Constitution, the House of Representatives shall function as the Diet until such time as the House of Councillors shall be constituted.

ARTICLE 102. The term of office for half the members of the House of Councillors serving in the first term under this Constitution shall be three years. Members falling under this category shall be determined in accordance with law.

ARTICLE 103. The Ministers of State, members of the House of Representatives, and judges in office on the effective date of this Constitution, and all other public officials who occupy positions corresponding to such positions as are recognized by this Constitution, shall not forfeit their positions automatically on account of the enforcement of this Constitution unless otherwise specified by law. When, however, successors are elected or appointed under the provisions of this Constitution they shall forfeit their positions as a matter of course.

Date of Promulgation: November 3, 1946.
Date of Enforcement: May 3, 1947.

Selected Bibliography

Bisson, Thomas Arthur, *Prospects for Democracy in Japan*, New York, Macmillan, 1949.

Burks, Ardath W., *The Government of Japan*, University Paperbacks, Methuen, 2nd edition, London, 1964.

Ike, Nobutaka, *The Beginnings of Political Democracy in Japan*, Baltimore, John Hopkins Press, 1950.

Johnstone, William C., *The Future of Japan*, Oxford University Press, New York, 1945.

Maki, John M., *Government and Politics in Japan*, Thames and Hudson, London, 1962.

Martin, Edwin M., *The Allied Occupation of Japan*, New York, Institute of Pacific Relations, 1948.

Maruyama, Masao, *Thought and Behaviour in Modern Japanese Politics*, Ed. by Ivan Morris. London, Oxford University Press, 1963.

McNelly, Theodore, *Contemporary Government of Japan*, George Allen and Unwin Ltd., London, 1963.

Munro, W. B. and Arearst Morley, *The Government of Europe*, 4th edition, The Macmillan Company, New York, 1963.

Ministry of Foreign Affairs, Japan, *Japan in Transition* (One Hundred Years of Modernisation), 1968.

Norman, E. Herbert, *Japan's Emergence as a Modern State*, New York, Institute of Pacific Relations, 1940.

Quigley, Harold S. and Turner, John E., *The New Japan*, Oxford University Press, London, 1956.

Scalapino, Robert A., *Democracy and the Party Movement in Prewar Japan*, Berkeley, University of California Press, 1953.

Story, Richard, *A History of Modern Japan*, Middlesex, Harmondsworth, Penguin Books, 1960.

UNESCO, *Post War Democratisation in Japan*, Paris, 1961 (International Social Science Journal, Vol. 13.)

Ward, Robert E., *Japan's Political System*, Prentice-Hall, New Jersey, 1967.

118   *Parliamenlary Democracy in Japan*

Yanaga, Chitoshi, *Japanese People and Politics*, John Wiley &
Sons, New York, 1956.
Yoshida, Shigeru, *The Yoshida Memoirs: The Story of Japan in
Crisis*. Tr. by Ken'ichi Yoshida, London, Heinemann, 1961.
Japan's Decisive Century: 1867-1967, New York, F. A.
Praeger, 1967.

Articles

Ike, Nobutaka, *Japan, Jwenty Years after Surrender*, Asian Survey
6 (January, 1966) 18-27.
Jean Pearce, *Japan's Komei Party May Split from Buddhist Move-
ment*, *Amrita Bazar Patrika*, February 2, 1970.
Matsuo, Taka yo shi, "The Development of Democracy in
Japan", *Developing Economics*, December 4, 1966.
Nakamura, Koji, "Emergence of a New Militarism in Japan,"
Amrita Bazar Patrika, May 20, 1970.
"New Lease for U. S.-Japan Security Pact", *Amrita Bazar
Patrika*, June 24, 1970.
New York Times, "Japan Steps into New Decade with Self-
confidence," *Amrita Bazar Patrika*, January 24, 1970.
Nobuhiko Ushiba, "Some Thoughts on the 1970s", published
by Public Information Bureau, Ministry of Foreign Affairs,
Tokyo, Japan (Reference Series No. 5-69, code No. 12110.)
Sivapali Wickremasinghe, "Japan's Fringe Party Komeito,"
Amrita Bazar Patrika, June 3, 1969.
Sulzberger, C. L., "Japan's Sun also Rises," *Amrita Bazar
Patrika*, August 14, 1970.
Takashi oka, "Japan's Revived Self Confidence," *Amrita Bazar
Patrika*, January 14, 1970.
Yamamura, Kozo, "Growth Vs. Economic Democracy in Japan:
1945-1965," *Journal of Asian Studies*, August, 1966, 713-728.
Ward, Robert E., "The Origins of the Present Japanese
Constitution," *American Political Science Review* (1956).

Index

Administrative tribunals, 67
Akihito (Crown Prince), 36
American Constitution, 15, 27
American House of Representatives, 52-3
Asia, 48, 85-6
Asian Development Bank, 86
Asquith (Lord), 34
Austria, 2
Autonomy Ministry, 93-4
Ballot, 72
Bill of Rights (American), 73
Board of Audit, 40, 57
Britain, 16, 25, 32-3, 35, 37, 56
British Cabinet, 39
British Constitution, 33-4
British Courts, 70
British monarch, 31-2, 34
British Parliament, 48, 71
British Prime Minister, 45
British Queen, 32-5, 63
British Speaker, 53
Budget, 42, 45, 48, 57, 60
Cabinet, 14, 32, 48, 51, 65, 70
 —collective responsibility of, 38-40
 —composition of, 40-2
 —functions of, 42-4
China (Communist), 86-8
Chou En-lai, 21
Churchill, 13, 25
Communist Party, 82, 84-5, 87
Congress of the United States, 48, 55-6
Constituent Assembly, 59
Constitution of 1889, 23, 29, 32, 35, 37-9, 44, 58, 90
Court of Administrative Litigation, 67
Councillors, 50-1
Daisaku Ikeda, 82
Democratic Party, 82
Democratic Socialist Party, 82-4

Democracy, 29
Dicey, 67
Diet, 12, 14-6, 32, 39-42, 48-61, 93
 —qualifications of the members of, 51-2
 —immunities of the members of, 53-4
 —committees of, 54-6
 —session of, 54
 —functions of, 56-9
 —relation between the two Houses of, 59-61
Direct Democracy, 15-7
Disciplinary Committee, 53
District Courts, 62, 64
East Asia, 28
England, 42
Emperor, 23-36, 48, 62-3
English monarchy, 26
Family Courts, 62, 64-5
Far East, 85-6
Federal Assembly (Swiss), 54
Federal Council (Swiss), 54
Federal Tribunal (Swiss), 64, 71
Formosa, 87
France, 25, 67
Fundamental human rights, 17
George V (King), 36
High Courts, 62, 64
Hirano, 45
Hirohito (Emperor), 8, 25-6, 28-9, 31
Hirokawa, 45
Hokkaido, 91
House of Representatives, 14, 27, 32, 43, 49, 52, 57, 59-60, 68, 84-5
House of Commons, 33-4, 46, 52-3, 56
House of Councillors, 43, 50, 59-60
House of Lords, 60
House of Peers, 61
Hume (Lord), 33

119

Impeachment Court, 58, 70
Imperial Diet, 48, 58
Imperial House, 35, 57
Imperial Party, 80
Indian Constitution, 11, 15
Inferior Courts, 64-5
Inukai, 81
Itagaki, 80
Ito, 80
Joint Committee, 60
Judiciary, 62-72
— independence of, 69-70
Judicial review, 70-2
Jun'ye yano, 89
Katayama, 45, 82
Kazuo, 11
Keiki, 2
Kenzo, Takayanagi, 18
Kishi Nobusuke, 82
Komeito, 82, 85, 88-9
Konoye, Fumimaro, 25, 28
Kurile islands, 88
Kyoto, 91
Liberal Democratic Party, 52, 80-3, 85-6
Liberal Party, 80, 82
Legal Research and Training Institute, 70
Legislative Committee, 55
Local Autonomy Law, 92
Macmillan, 33
MacArthur, 18, 21, 26, 44, 52
Margaret, 33
Meiji (Emperor), 2, 8, 25, 36
Meiji Restoration, 90
Nakamura, Koji, 21
National Council (Swiss), 54
Nichiren, 82
Nishio Suehiro, 83
Nixon (President), 85
Netherlands, 25
North Korea, 20-1
North Vietnam, 20
Nuclear Non-Proliferation Treaty, 22
Okinawa, 85
Okuma, 80

Osaka, 91
Parliament (British) Act, 1911, 60
Patriotic Public Party, 80
Peoples' Republic of China, 20
Popular Sovereignty, 10-3
Potsdam Declaration, 4, 13
Prefecture, 51-2
President of India, 42, 69
President (U. S.), 58, 64
Prime Minister, 44-7, 57, 63
Prince Philip, 33
Procurator-general, 65
Prussia, 2
Public Procurators, 65-6, 70
Referendum, 59
Reform Party, 80
Renunciation of war, 17-22
Rhodesia, 33
Roosevelt, 19
Rule of Law, 67
Sato Eisaku, 85-6
Secularism, 75
Security Treaty between Japan and the U. S., 19, 21-2, 55, 60, 84-7
Senate (U. S.), 58, 60
Separation of powers, 72
Socialist Party, 82, 85-7
Social Democratic Party, 83
Sokagakkai, 82-3
Soviet Constitution, 13
Soviet Union, 20, 28, 71, 88
Speaker, 52-4
Steering Committee, 55
Summary Courts, 62, 64
Supreme Court (U. S.) 64, 71-2
Supreme Court (U. S. S. R.), 71
Supreme Court (India), 69
Supreme Court (Japan), 32, 43, 62
— composition of, 63
— qualifications of the judges of, 63
— method of appointment of the judges of, 63
— chief judge of, 63
Swiss Constitution, 15
Switzerland, 54, 71
Takeiri, 88-9

Taiwan, 87
Tokyo, 62, 87, 91
Tokugawa government, 2
Truman, 13
United Nations, 30, 86-7
United Kingdom, 39
United States, 4, 11, 19, 22, 25-7, 30,
    37, 42, 44, 54-6, 58, 60, 64, 81
Universal adult suffrage, 16, 75
Universal Suffrage Act, 1925, 52

Ushiba Nobuhiko, 22, 87
Vice-Speaker, 52
Victoria (Queen), 35
Vice-Minister, 41
Vice-Premier, 44-5
Vice-President of the U. S., 45
World War II, 3, 21, 28
Yoshida, 45
Yomiuri, 86

DATE DUE
